# THE SERMON ON THE MOUNT

# THE SERMON ON THE MOUNT

## THE DIRECTORY
## OF THE DEVOUT LIFE

BY

## F. B. MEYER

**BAKER BOOK HOUSE**
**GRAND RAPIDS 6, MICHIGAN**
1959

Reprinted, 1959, by
BAKER BOOK HOUSE

Reprinted from the original
printing made in 1904 under
the title, *The Directory of
the Devout Life.*

PHOTOLITHOPRINTED BY CUSHING - MALLOY, INC.
ANN ARBOR, MICHIGAN, UNITED STATES OF AMERICA
1959

# Preface.

THERE is too much of mere sentiment and emotion in what goes by the name of religion, and too little practical Christian living. The tree is not good, the inward parts are not thoroughly cleansed, the rule of Christ is not absolutely dominant in speech and life. People are willing enough to accept freely a forgiveness which He purchased by His blood, but are slow to believe that He is a King, whose law must be obeyed in its jots and tittles.

We can never allow the great objective facts of Christianity, and their attendant doctrines, to sink low on our horizon; but we must give equal prominence to the demands of Christ for a righteousness which shall exceed that of the Scribes and Pharisees, and a perfection which shall resemble that of God. We have no right to be content with saying " Lord, Lord;" we must do the things which He says.

In my earliest days I was reared in a school that loved the "juicy" doctrines of Grace, and if a sermon were preached from our pulpit which laid special stress on Christian ethics, during our walk home it would be dismissed as Luther dismissed the general Epistle of James, as "right strawy," and as savouring too much of the moral essay and too little of the Gospel. It seemed as though some of the audience were a little afraid of

Christ as a teacher of morals, whilst willing enough to recognise Him as Saviour.

We understand the matter better now, and have learnt that those who would ascend the Hill of the Lord, and stand in His holy place, must have clean hands and pure hearts, must not lift up their souls to vanity nor swear deceitfully.

Of course, the right kind of obedience is impossible, apart from the Cross and the Spirit. We must be reconciled before we can become obedient children; we must be filled with the Spirit before " the fragrance of Christ " can be manifested through us in every place. The Sermon on the Mount must be read in the transfiguring light which shines backwards from the later events in our Lord's life.

When, however, this is borne in mind, each sentence of that marvellous discourse glistens with celestial radiance, and rings with the music of the Gospel. In such a spirit let us address ourselves to the study of the " Directory of the Devout Life," as it is contained in Matt. v., vi., and vii.

*F. B. Meyer.*

# Contents.

# Introductory.

(MATT. v. 1, 2.)

ACCOMPANIED by His newly-acquired disciples, our Lord had travelled throughout Galilee, hastening from place to place, from one synagogue to another. Everywhere He proclaimed the Glad Tidings of the Kingdom, and accompanied the preaching by mighty deeds. He healed the sick and cast out demons, dispelling every form of infirmity and disease which He encountered in His triumphal progress. On the sunlit path of the Prince of Life all the sad results of human sin fled, as the wreathed mists of morning before sunrise.

It was a morning without clouds. His fame spread far and near throughout all Syria. The people, who, between the exactions of the Pharisees and the hair-splitting of the Scribes, were like harried sheep, welcomed His advent with a great outburst of joy. On the one hand, He was so accessible in His sympathy; on the other, so transcendent in His purity and grace. A general impulse of hope and expectation was diffused abroad, and they sought out all who were sick and diseased in mind and body, to bring them into His gracious and health-giving presence. In addition to these crowds of sympathisers and friends were groups of curiosity-mongers and sightseers, of inquirers and devout souls, who followed Him, with a great expectancy in their hearts, from Decapolis, Jerusalem, Judæa, and beyond Jordan.

When He saw the crowds increasing thus, He felt that He must withdraw temporarily from their presence. He could not permit the seasons of holy fellowship with His Father to be broken in upon even by eager appeals for sympathy and healing. Besides, He had reached a decisive moment in His career, when, as His answer to the increasing malice of the leaders of Judaism, it became necessary to organize His followers, and secure the consolidation and perpetuation of His work. A forward step was to be taken, which demanded that He should give Himself to prolonged intercessory prayer, so that He might do nothing of Himself, but only what He saw His Father doing. He was to choose the men whose names, long afterwards, were to be engraven on the foundation stones of the New Jerusalem. He must, therefore, give Himself to prayer.

The scene of this midnight vigil, and afterwards of the Sermon on the Mount, is an upland rather than a mountain, which rises to about a thousand feet above the level of the sea, and is distinctly marked out from neighbouring eminences by the two horns which crown its summit.

Let us follow the Master's steps, as He ascended by a long and easy slope of unfenced common land, the grass of which was embroidered with daisies, white and red anemones, blue hyacinths, and the yellow-flowered clover, and on which the brown cattle browsed. After a gradual ascent of three or four miles, He reached at length a great crater-like space, with a slightly hollow floor, set in a frame of rough crags, and strewn with boulders and fragments of black basalt—as if they had been rained on the earth in a terrific shower (Dr. Geikie). Above, the hill rose up into two high grassy knolls, some sixty feet in height, known as the Horns of Hattin. This is the spot, so tradition says, where the Master continued all night in prayer to God. He may have selected for His oratory the summit of one of those grassy knolls, whilst the disciples occupied some lower ridge; and at dawn the people began to gather from the neighbouring villages, where they had spent the night, to crowd the vast audience-chamber, hollowed out as an amphitheatre below. On the south-west, the huge cone of Tabor; to the north, the majestic snow-crowned summit of Hermon; below to the east, the glittering waters of the lake; far away on its other side, the precipitous cliffs of Gadara, rising sheer from its shores; no signs of human habitation; no sound of earthly toil; no fear of intrusion, save from the feathered and furred denizens of air and earth, the free pensioners with the lilies on His Father's care—such was the oratory, whose soft grass was trodden by those blessed feet, or indented by that kneeling form.

It was on the mountain, as Luke tells us, that He prayed (Luke vi. 12, 13). As the dawn broke over the hills, He *called* His disciples from their slumbers, and chose from them twelve, that they might be with Him, and that He might send them forth to preach, and to have authority to cast out demons (Mark iii. 13–15). He then appears to have sat down, after the recognised Eastern fashion, opened His mouth, and taught (Matt. v. 1, 2). Through paragraph after paragraph, which were to mould the minds of men after a new fashion, and influence the course of coming centuries more powerfully than those of Plato and Aristotle, His speech moved with the transparency and brightness of the River of Life, which proceedeth from the throne of God and of the Lamb. Then, descending with His chosen band of Apostles, and accompanied by the rest of His disciples, He came down to the level place where the vast congregation was awaiting Him; and lifting up His eyes with special tenderness on the inner circle, but in tones audible to the furthest extremities of the crowd, He repeated in a shorter form the marvellous discourse which He had already delivered (Luke vi. 17–38).

This discourse, laying the foundation of the Kingdom of Heaven, may also be called the Directory of the Devout Life, and we can wish for nothing better than to drink into its spirit, and realize its exquisite ideals. Whilst it is, in a literal sense, "the Sermon on the Mount," because uttered on one of the great natural altars of the world, may it not be called so in the symbolical and metaphorical case? Our Lord was standing on the very summit of spiritual experience. His own soul was fragrant with the Beatitudes which He uttered for His disciples. He possessed in living human experience all that He inculcated. With exquisite naturalness and simplicity, He was describing His own experiences, was revealing the secrets of His deepest nature, and was delineating in colours that can never fade the features of His own face. From the heights, He was calling to men in the lowlands of error and sin, to summon them to His own standpoint. This is emphatically the sermon of the mountain heights.

. . . . . .

The close similarity and contrast between this sermon and the giving of the Law from Sinai, has often been discussed, and we need do no more than note the points that have been made. *There*, the great prophet of the Old Covenant received God's Law by the mediation of angels, and his feelings must have been elevated far above their ordinary level ; *here*, the Prophet of the New Covenant utters the revelation of God from the depths of His own heart, from the matured experiences of His own habitual condition. *There*, the Law was accompanied by the roll of thunder and the blinding lightning flash ; *here*, the accompaniments were soft breezes, the blue canopy of heaven, the lilies, and the birds of the air. *There*, the Law was written on tablets of stone ; *here*, on the fleshy tablets of the heart. *There*, the Laws were Prohibitions ; *here*, Beatitudes. *There*, the first tables of the Law were shattered because of the disobedience of the people, and the second form was equally stern and exacting ; *here*, out of tender compassion for the weakness of the people, our Lord repeats the sermon with a somewhat slighter texture. Moses constrained to obedience, by pronouncing the disobedient accursed ; whilst Christ attracts to loving loyalty, by pronouncing the blessedness of the citizens of His Kingdom. Men were not to be driven by terror, but attracted by winsomeness and sweet reasonableness.

This was the third discourse. The first had been to Nicodemus, the master in Israel, on the necessity of a spiritual union with God—this is the beginning of the devout life. The second had been to the unnamed woman at Sychar's well, on the nature of spiritual worship—this is the nurture of the devout life. The third is on the rule and direction of the healthy and holy soul—this may therefore be called the Directory of the Devout Life. It has been said that there is nothing of the Cross or of Pentecost in this discourse ; but each of them is required to transform these precepts into living and gracious experience. There must be, for each sinful soul, that forgiveness and cleansing which are possible only through the blood of the Cross, or it can never enter through the white gates of pearl into this city of God. For each, too, there must be the inbreathing of the new life—the being born again, not of corruptible seed, but of incorruptible—before that life can be cultured and moulded into the developments of which this Sermon gives outline and model.

" How," asks the disciple in one of old Jacob Behmen's treatises, " shall I be able so to live as not to lose the

eternal peace amid anxiety and tribulation?" To which
the Master answers: " If thou dost once every hour throw
thyself by faith beyond all creatures into the abysmal
mercy of God, into the sufferings of our Lord, and into
the fellowship of His intercession, and yieldest thyself fully
and absolutely thereto, thou shalt receive power from
above to rule over death and the devil, and to subdue
hell and the world under thee." Yes; and we may add,
then thou shalt be able to realize the noble ideal which
is presented in our Lord's incomparable Directory of the
Devout Life, as presented in these chapters.

# I

# Oh, the Blessedness!

### (PSA. xxxii. 1 ; MATT. v. 1–12.)

THERE is a condition of soul which may be experienced and enjoyed by every child of our race, which the Master calls Blessedness. He uses the same word to describe it as is employed to set forth the Being of God and the Life of the Saints who have passed beyond the vail.

" *Blessed are ye* " (Matt. v. 11).

" *The glorious Gospel of the Blessed God* " (1 Tim. i. 11).

" *Blessed are the dead which die in the Lord* " (Rev. xiv. 13).

This condition of soul, however, need not be postponed until we too, in our turn, pass the Gate of the City, and find ourselves amid "the solemn troops and sweet societies" of eternity. It may be entered here and now. The fragrance of this garden steals through the crowded and noisy cities of our modern civilization like the morning air laden with the scent of new-mown grass. The gates of this city stand open, night and day, for lonely souls, in country and sequestered places, where the noise of our city life cannot reach ; and at any moment they may tread its thronged streets, listen to its murmured speech, and join in its vast convocations, of which it is written : " Ye are come to Mount Sion, the City of the Living God, to myriads of angels, to the general assembly and church of the first-born."

.    .    .    .    .    .

Blessedness does not depend on outward possessions, such as worldly goods, or lands, or high birth, or erudite culture.

Indeed, there are words of Christ which suggest that they who stand possessed of these things will find it harder to enter that Paradise which has not yet faded from our world, and to pass through the gates of that city which are before our eyes, if only they were opened to discern them. When He repeated this Sermon of the Mountain-Heights and of the Dawn, to the multitudes that stood breathless beneath its spell, He said, "Woe unto you that are rich. . . . Woe unto you that are full. . . . Woe unto you, ye that laugh." He did not mean that such would be necessarily excluded, but that entrance into blessedness would be harder for them; as when, after dusk, a camel strives to get through the needle-eye-gate, placed in the city wall for belated pedestrians.

There is no soul of man so illiterate, so lonely, so poor in this world's goods, so beset with hereditary sins and demoniacal temptations, that may not at this moment step suddenly into this life of blessedness, begin to drink of the river which makes glad the city of God, the holy place of the tabernacles of the Most High. It is not necessary to ascend into Heaven to bring it down, or to descend into the Depth of the Abyss to bring it up; it has not to be wrestled or wept for; it is not to be obtained by the merit of holy deeds, or as the guerdon of devoted service; it is not a reward which comes after long years in the council chamber or on the tented field. We have not to do, or feel, or suffer, but only to be; to cultivate certain dispositions; to possess a nature, here carefully defined—and instantly blessedness begins, an unearthly light breaks on the soul, which is destined to increase into the full radiance of Heaven's high noon. "Come in, thou blessed of the Lord" (can you not hear the angel-voices?); "wherefore standest thou without?"

.        .        .        .        .        .

Our Master did not speak of this condition of soul by hearsay; for thirty years it had been His sweet and deep experience. During His life in Nazareth, had not the Lamb of God lain in His Father's bosom? Had He not realized that He was wrapped around with the love which had been His before the worlds were made? Had He not been content to let the great ones of the world go on their way of pomp and pride, because He was assured of a deeper joy, a more perfect peace, a more satisfying happiness, than Cæsar's smile or the Imperial purple could afford? The well of water was springing up in His own pure heart before He spoke of it to the woman at Sychar's well. He knew the Father, loved the Father, fulfilled His Father's behests, rested in the Father's will, was encompassed with the perpetual sense of the Father's presence, breathed the sunny air of the Father's love. During His earthly life, as He confessed Himself, the Son of Man was, therefore, already " in heaven " (John iii. 13). He offers us what He was experiencing for Himself. " *My* peace I leave with you; *My* peace I give unto you." " These things have I spoken unto you, that *My* joy might remain in you." "That the love wherewith Thou lovest *Me* may be in them."

Not to the same degree, but after the same quality and kind, we may know in this life, amid difficult, tempestuous, and sorrowful experiences, what the Lord felt when He said: " He that sent Me is with Me ; the Father hath not left Me alone, for I do always those things which please Him."

. . . . . .

THE INGREDIENTS OF THIS EXPERIENCE are enumerated thus :—

First, it is blessed *to belong to that invisible Kingdom* which is already in our world, including within its ever-

expanding circle all gracious souls of every race and age,
breathing the ozone of Heaven into the stale and exhausted
atmosphere of the world; its King, the Enthroned Lamb;
its subjects, the childlike, the forgiving, the gentle, and the
pure; its laws, love; its advances, soft, sweet, irresistible
as the dawn; its duration, eternal. It is a blessed thing
to know that one has the franchise and freedom of that
Kingdom, that one need never go out from its holy and
strong embrace, and that men like John the Divine may
greet us thus: "Your brother and partaker with you . . .
in the Kingdom, . . . which is in Jesus" (Rev. i. 9, R.V.).

2. Second, it is blessed *to be comforted with the comfort
which only God can give*. When the eyes are wet with
tears that refuse to be staunched, to feel a hand soft
and strong wiping them away, and to discover that it is
the Hand

> That can ruffle an evening calm,
> And bears Calvary's mark on its piercèd palm;

when the face is buried deep amid the dried flowers and
leaves of departed joys, to hear a whisper which thrills the
sense, growing fuller and clearer, like a flute, and to detect
in its syllables the assurances of the Comforter Himself;
when the sepulchre seems to hold all that made life worth
living, to become suddenly aware that there is a presence
near at hand, and to find that the Gardener Himself is at
hand to lift the drooping plant of life, unfurling its petals
again to the light; to be strong in God's strength, comforted with the paracletism of the Paraclete, to drink of
the brook by the way—here is blessedness which eye hath
not seen, neither the ear of ordinary man heard, nor the
unregenerate heart perceived. Even the bereaved and
lonely heart, sitting amid the wreckage of all its joys and
hopes, may be aware of this.

3. Third, it is blessed *to inherit the earth*. When that

condition of soul is reached of which the Master is speaking,

> Heaven above is softer blue,
> Earth around is sweeter green ;
> Something shines in every hue
> Christless eyes have never seen.

There is a new rapture in common sights, a new meaning in common sounds; lilies are robed more sumptuously than Solomon ; the winged and furred denizens of the woodlands become, as St. Francis found them, " little brothers and sisters." As Cowper said, such a man may be poor compared with those whose mansions glitter in his sight, but he calls the luxuriant prospect all his own. Every wind wafts him blessing ; all things work together for his good. Whether Paul, or Apollos, or Cephas, or the world, or life, or death, or things present, or things to come—all things bring their tribute to the man who has learnt Christ's secret, which, like the fabled philosopher's stone, turns everything into gold. What inheriting the earth means is shown in the words of one of Christ's most proficient pupils, when he said : " I have learned in whatsoever state I am therewith to be content." You may own vast estates, and get nothing from them. You may have no rod or perch of land, and yet you may derive joy and delight from every scene, and extract nutriment from every incident. Newspapers, public events, journals, travels, pictures, architecture, literature, human life—all shall minister to your joy and perfecting.

4. Fourth, it is blessed *to be filled*. In this life, as well as in the next, it is possible to hunger no more, neither thirst any more. Not to hunger for the husks that the swine eat, because filled with the provisions of the Father's table ! Not to thirst for the heated pools at which the children of the world seek to quench their thirst, because the well of

water, that springs up to eternal life, is within! Not to clamour for the fleshpots of Egypt, because there is so plentiful a provision of manna. Oh, it is a blessed thing to be filled with the Spirit, to be full of joy and peace, to be fulfilled with God's grace and heavenly benediction, to be filled with the fruits of righteousness, to be filled with the knowledge of His will, to be filled unto the fulness of God. Tennyson says that the babble of the Wye among the hills lasts until the tidal wave fills up its channels to the brim; and the heart is restless till it is full—but when it has realized this blessed fulness, dipped deep into the fulness of God, and lifted out dripping with flashing drops, ah, then, evil has no lure to charm, the fear of man cannot intrude, the fascination and blandishments of sense are neutralized. What more can the soul want than to be filled with Thee, O God, who didst make us for Thyself? Cannot a flower be satisfied which has a sun to shine on it, and a glacier-fed river to wash its roots?

Fifth, it is blessed _to be the recipient of mercy_. There is never a moment of our life in which we do not stand in need of mercy, both at the hands of our fellows, and, above all, from the hand of God. There is no saint in the heavenly Kingdom who does not, at some time or other, need to appropriate the petitions of the man after God's own heart, and say: "Have mercy on me, O God, according to Thy loving-kindness, according to the multitude of Thy tender mercies."

We need mercy from little children, startled by our harsh tones; mercy from our servants and employés, hindered by our inconsistencies, our quick temper and imperious tones; mercy from husband or wife, brother or sister, neighbour or friend—above all, mercy from the Most Merciful; and it is blessed to know that we have it in Heaven's own measure, full, pressed down, and running over. So far from it making us lax in permitting sin, it predisposes us to more mercy towards the failings of others, more mercilessness to ourselves.

Sixth, it is blessed *to have the vision of God*. Not to terrify, as when Moses hid his face, and Elijah went into the covert of the cave, and John fell at His feet as dead; but more after the fashion of Mr. Hewitson's experience, when he says: "Our Redeemer is no mere abstraction, no ideality that has its being only in our shifting thoughts—He is the most personal of all persons, the most living of all who live. He is 'the First and the Last, and the Living One.' He is so near us, as the Son of God, that we can feel His warm breath on our souls; and, as the Son of Man, He has a heart like these hearts of ours—a human heart, meek and lowly, tender, kind, and sympathizing. In the Word—the almost *viva voce* utterance of Himself—His arm of power is stretched forth beside you, that you may lean on it with all your weight; and in the Word, also, His love is revealed, that on the bosom of it you may lay your aching head, and forget your sorrow in the abundance of His consolation. To the Living One who died we must look, that we may be weaned and won over to God, that we may be strengthened, spiritualized, and sanctified." Who would not desire a life like this, in which God should be the one dear Presence, the one familiar and ever-present object of thought, the Friend with whom an increasing dialogue is maintained? A young girl employed in a shop told me the other day that her consciousness of God and her converse with Him had now lasted for three years, and that difficult things had become easy, as though He arranged all and smoothed out the creases.

Seventh, it is blessed *to be recognised as the son of God*. Some are undoubtedly children of God, who are not like God. It would require a good deal of scrutiny to detect

His image and superscription on their faces, or the tones of His voice in their speech. The manners of the Heavenly Court are not evident in their demeanour; the courtesy and thoughtfulness that characterised the Son are not characteristic of their behaviour to the poor and timid, to little children and women. They too often break the bruised reed, and quench the smoking flax; they strive and cry and cause their voices to be heard in the street; they do not bear, believe, hope, and endure all things, or elicit the love of men to Him whose name and nature they ought to bear in every lineament. Be it ours to be imitators of God as dear children, to be harmless and blameless, the sons of God, without rebuke—to be thus is to be blessed.

Eighth, *we come back to the Kingdom of Heaven*. For blessedness is like a spiral staircase, we are always coming back to the same standpoint from a higher position on the circling round. When we begin to live for God we find ourselves in the Kingdom, and are ravished with the beauty of the dawn; but after years have been spent in doing His will, and walking in His fellowship, there is a new depth of loveliness and significance in its infinite and Divine contents.

O Christ, Thou King of Glory, uplift us above the common dusty road of mortal life—lift us into Thy life, above the heads of our enemies, above the weight of our flesh, above the glamour of the world, and make us most blessed for ever, and glad with joy in Thy presence!

# II

# The Passive Side of the Blessed Life.

LET us study our Lord's ideal of character with the prayer that He would graciously repeat it in us, and that He would be in us that which He commends; for it is only as He gives us Himself, in all the fulness of His perfected manhood, that we can *apprehend* that for which we were *apprehended*, and be that which He desires. Do you realize this, my reader? Have you made room for Him, and are you allowing Him to possess you wholly, till He becomes in very deed *your life*? The vine must abide in the branch, or these fruits will be impossible. " Apart from Him, . . . *nothing*."

To be *poor in spirit* is to be vacant of self and waiting for God. To have no confidence in the flesh; to be emptied of self-reliance; to be conscious of absolute insufficiency; to be thankfully dependent on the life-energy of the living God—that is poverty of spirit; and it has been characteristic of some of the noblest, richest, most glorious natures that have ever trodden the shores of Time. Happy are they who are conscious of a poverty which only the Divine indwelling can change into wealth, and who are willing, like the wondrous beggar of Meister Eckhart, to confess that they would rather be in hell and have God, than in heaven and not have Him.

It is, indeed, remarkable that some of the most richly dowered in mental and moral wealth have been most eager to confess that they were nothing—babes in the world of

being, children picking up stones on the shores of boundless
oceans, scholars on the lowest form of the school, to whom
mature growth and knowledge seemed as yet indefinitely
distant.

The way to become poor in spirit is to realize that thou
hast no power of thine own by which to bless and help
others, and to open thy whole being to the incoming and
through-flowing of the wealth of the ever-blessed God.    It
was thus that the Master Himself lived and wrought.
Though He was rich in all the Divine plenitude of His
Divine nature, "He became poor," "and emptied Himself."
In other words, He determined not to speak His own
words, follow His own scheme and plan, or work His
mighty works in His own might ; but became the channel
and instrument through which His Father spoke, wrought,
and reconciled the world unto Himself.   O soul of man,
there is no other course for thee and me !   Not to draw up
the water with which to quench men's thirst from the
marshes of our own souls, but to be channels through which
the river of God may flow, as the water of far-away lakes is
brought to the myriads of our great cities.   To confess that
thou art nothing, but that Christ is all ;. to know that thou
canst do nothing effective to bless men, but that Christ
can, and will, do it by thee—that is the secret of this
poverty of spirit which unlocks the treasures of the kingdom of heaven.

Many ancient authorities place *meekness* next, and it
seems the natural order, for the soul that realizes its own
nothingness and helplessness is likely to be meek.   The
meek are so occupied with their desire that God's grace
should pass through them to their fellows, that they are
prepared to sink all considerations of their own standing
and position, so long as nothing may interfere with the
effect for which they long.   Their only thought is to carry

their point, to bless men who do not want to be blessed, to vanquish hate by love, and rebellion by loving-kindness and tender mercy. They cannot afford, therefore, to be always standing on their own dignity, and defending their own rights. These are willingly cast into the furnace to augment the flame, that the obdurate metal may be fused. "Being reviled, we bless; being persecuted, we endure; being defamed, we entreat. We are made as the filth of the world, the offscouring of all things; but all things are for your sakes, that the abundant grace through the thanksgiving of many may abound to the glory of God."

The way to become meek is to be absorbingly taken up with the love of Christ for men. Be lowly before God, allowing His love to enter and fill thy heart, and thou wilt find it easy to be meek towards man. Thy pride will be driven out by the expulsive power of the new affection. Thou wilt be prepared to accept flouts and sneers, if only thou canst bless and help others; even as God, who answers not the blasphemous and hard things that are said against Him, but continues to send His rain and causes His sun to shine, that He may bring men back in penitence to His heart.

It would be a great mistake, however, to suppose that the meek are cowardly, deficient in strength of purpose or force of will: they are among the strongest and most strenuous of men. Always they are strong in patience, and strenuous in seeking the salvation of others. Let the cause of righteousness, justice, or truth be in question, none are so unbending or stalwart as they. Of the wrongs done to themselves, they are disposed to take no count; but they dare not refrain from bearing witness, both by speech and act, whenever the sacred majesty of truth is assailed, and in danger of being trampled under foot.

It is natural that the meek should become those that

_mourn_. They feel keenly the evil of sin and the sanctity of sorrow; like Him who sighed as He touched the tongue of the dumb, groaned as He came to the grave of His friend, and wept as He beheld the city.

Of all mourners, Jeremiah is one of the most plaintive. There is no lyric on the page of history to be compared with the Book of Lamentations :—

"_Mine eye runneth down with rivers of water._"

"_Mine eye poureth down and ceaseth not._"

"_Mine eye affecteth my soul._"

But as we turn from the sin of the world, the woes of men, the high-handed wrong of the great, and the abject poverty, sorrow, and anguish of heart of the oppressed, to the sin of our own hearts, the broken ideals, the frustrated purposes, the perpetual contrast between what we would be and what we are, surely our tears must have more salt in them, and cut deeper courses in their flow.

There is surely no need to show the steps towards mourning such as this. Look above thee and see the Christ stand, so pure, so chaste, so glorious in the light in which He arrays Himself as with a garment, and thou wilt abhor thyself and repent in the dust. Look around thee, and try to estimate the weight of a world's apostasy, the deluge of tears, the hurricane of sighs, that mount up to heaven. "Ah, it's a sair world, my masters!"

But the mourners are not content to shed tears only, _they hunger and thirst after righteousness._ St. Augustine says that they hunger and thirst after the Righteous One —"Jesus Christ the Righteous." They were made for Him, and will never be satisfied until they attain to the fruition of all their hopes, to know Him, and the power of His resurrection, and the fellowship of His sufferings.

Without doubt, such is their supreme desire; and, as included in this, they hunger and thirst for the ultimate triumph of righteousness in their own hearts and in the world of men. Every moan of pain, every consciousness of failure, every temporary triumph of reactionary and destructive forces—elicits the more urgent and persistent prayer, "Thy Kingdom come." The personal coming of the Lord is desired not, primarily, because the Bride desires the Bridegroom; but because the subject longs for the triumph of that Kingdom, which is righteousness, joy, and peace in the Holy Ghost.

This aspiration is noble. Some hungers are ignoble, despicable, and base. But this is shared in by God Himself, whose Spirit longs with inexpressible desire to bring to an end the present condition of things, in the vindication and manifestation of His sons. The angels, as they behold the evil and pain of our earth; the champion of the rights of men, who wrestles with the hydra-headed and protean evil of his age; the wronged womanhood of the harem and the street; the dumb creation, groaning and travailing with enormous and cruel wrongs—all join in this blessed hunger and thirst, this aspiration which amounts to a sure and certain hope that cannot be ashamed.

Thou needest not be taught this, for thou hast often felt it. Amid the violet light of a dying summer's day, when soft and lovely music—songs without words—is filling the entranced and listening air, when some heroic stand for liberty is drowned and quenched in blood, when the white robes of the soul have been stained and polluted by some recent fall—then the soul hungers with an intolerable pain, and thirsts, as the wounded hart for water-brooks, that righteousness should set up its blessed and all-conquering reign.

## III.

# The Active Side of the Blessed Life.

### (MATT. v. 1–12.)

LET us now turn to the active side of the Blessed Life. *The merciful* are not content with bearing wrong; they pity the wrong-doer, pity him with a great compassion, because they realize that the heart which inflicts wrong must itself be tortured by remorse, scourged with the whips of the Furies, and certain to have an even more terrible awakening to shame and everlasting contempt. The merciful, therefore, go forth with a great longing to deliver the evildoer from himself.

It was thus that the Master felt when He bore the sins of His murderers in His own body on the tree, prayed for their forgiveness, and from His throne of glory sent the Spirit to turn the hearts of fathers to their children, and of the disobedient to the wisdom of the just.

The eyes of mercy are deep with compassionate glances, full of tears, the homes of prayer; the feet of mercy are soft in their tread, for they will not break the bruised reed, nor quench the smouldering spark in the dimly-burning flax; the voice of mercy is generous to the fallen, gentle to the weak, and gracious to the offender; from the heart of mercy, soothing balm flows to the wounds of sinners, of sufferers, and of the world.

The only way in which thou canst become merciful is to remember how much mercy thou needest and hast obtained. "Seeing," said the Apostle, "that we have obtained mercy, we faint not." Ah, think of the ten

thousand talents that have been forgiven thee, and thou
wilt not take thy brother by the throat and demand the
hundred pence in which he is a defaulter. Hast thou
forgotten the moment when thou heardest thy Lord say:
"Thy sins, which were many, are all forgiven thee"; and
art thou going to resent the approach of a sinful soul,
which loathes the miserable past, and longs to be emanci-
pated from the burden of unforgiven sin? Remember
thine own exceeding bitter cry which God has recorded in
His book: "Have mercy upon me, O God, according to Thy
loving-kindness: according unto the multitude of Thy
tender mercies."

The divinely merciful become, in the very nature of
things, the pure in heart. They have come to estimate by
their own inner experiences, and by the long effort which
the inveterate sin of others has demanded, how terrible and
horrible a thing sin is. The mother who has nursed one of
her children through some loathsome and painful disease
is filled with horror at it, and will take extravagant pre-
cautions to ward off the least germ or microbe that
menaces her home. Only those who have been forgiven
again and again, and who have forgiven, are quick to
discern the first symptom of impurity, and to turn from it
with shuddering horror. Yes; and to know what sin costs
to those that have to deliver the sinner, is such a revelation
of the bitter suffering of the Redeemer, that, in view of
what impurity costs Him, the soul flees from every taint of
uncleanness, lest it should add one pang more to that heart
which is already pierced through with many sorrows.

The way to purity is by Love. Wouldst thou be pure,
love Christ best of all, and love sinful men with a great
pity; and love shall be in thee like a fire. It is said that,
when Adam and Eve were created and lived in Eden,
they needed no garment of any kind, because their native

innocence emitted rays of light which enswathed their persons as an atmosphere. As much may be said of love, for where it fills the heart it sheds forth light and fire, which proceed from the very centre of our being, as the fire of God in the midst of the burning bush.

The pure in heart are naturally *the peacemakers*, because they cannot rest satisfied that the world of men should remain alienated from the life and holiness of God. They become, therefore, messengers of peace and benediction, seeking to reconcile between God and man, or between man and man, which is a most needful work, if ever the wrongs of time are to be righted, and earth become the home of love.

The way to this is to ask God to tell thee what work He is doing in the world, and whether thou mayest be permitted to help Him. He will tell thee that, having laid the foundations of peace in the Cross, He is going on to reconcile all things to Himself, whether they be in heaven, or on earth, or under the earth; and if thou wouldst have fellowship with Him, thou must set thyself to deal with all that breaks peace in thyself and in others.

Often in their prayers God's servants ask Him to *help* them. Without doubt the phrase can be abundantly justified; but does it not suggest that God is to shape His activities to the mould of *our* schemes, and accompany *us* along *our* chosen path? Is it not better to realize that all the burden and responsibility rest upon Him who is mighty; and that all working, whether to will or do, must emanate from Him as the fountain, and pass through us as the channel—submerging us as it passes forth to its blessed and victorious end?

Pre-eminently God is entitled "the God of Peace." He is ever engaged in healing the wounds and reconciling the enmities of the world. As nature covers the battlefield with golden harvests, so does God seek to undo the results of feud and strife, and lay foundations of justice for the temple of peace. Blessed indeed are they whom He associates with Himself in such pacific ministries.

But all such become *persecuted* and hated. It cannot be otherwise, apparently, in such a world as this. To have fellowship with the Lamb, we must have fellowship in His rejection and suffering. The servant is not above his Lord, and therefore the Master said sadly : " Ye shall indeed drink of My cup, and be baptized with the baptism that I am baptized with."

It is impossible to follow the Lord closely, and not be bespattered by the mud that was cast at Him. Indeed, to miss it may fill us with questionings. The soldier who follows the colonel through the thick of the fight will almost certainly have some scar to carry to his after years. We must see to it that all the evil is said against us falsely, and that we are reproached for the name of Christ. Is this thine experience ? Be of good cheer. Thou art on the track bedewed by the tears and blood of the martyrs of Jesus, and as they overcame so shalt thou. Be thou faithful unto death, and He shall give thee a crown of life. But through all thou shalt have a secret joy, a secret supply of strength, and a sweet intimacy with Him who before Pontius Pilate witnessed the good confession.

It should be noticed that these Beatitudes run in a parallel line with 1 Cor. xiii., and show what Love can be and do.

Poverty in spirit is Love in her chosen garb of humility, for she vaunteth not herself, and is not puffed up. Meekness is Love in the presence of wrong. Mourning is Love in tears. Hunger is Love's appetite. Mercy is Love on her errands of beneficence. Purity is Love on fire. Peacemaking is Love's effort to adjust the wrong of the world.

Persecution is Love's requital at the hands of those whom she would help. And Love is all this, intensely, perennially, constantly, because she cannot help it. Character has been defined as being what a man is in the dark : and Love is all this, not for fee or reward, not for notoriety or advertisement, but because she cannot be other. To be this is to be herself.

But who is sufficient for these things ? How can they be originated and perpetuated ? What is their nutriment and support ? There is but one reply. The Holy Spirit must come upon thee, and overshadow thee ; Christ must be formed in thee ; Heaven must descend to thee before it can shine out from thee.

It is affirmed that the evangelical side of religion is lacking in the Sermon on the Mount, but surely it is implied. The broad, much-trodden road foretells the great city whither it leads, and these wonderful chapters inevitably conduct to Calvary and the Upper Room.

Let a man seek to attain to Christ's ideal, and he will discover the infinite disparity between its crystal heights and his ineffectual efforts to clamber to their majestic crest ; he will need the propitiation and cleansing of the Blood of the Cross ; he will confess to the weakness and impotence of the Flesh ; he will lie at the feet of the Crucified as one dead, until the life of His resurrection enters to infill, indwell, and empower.

There is no hope of our being able to realize this exquisite portraiture by imitation or even by meditation. No ; He who originally conceived this ideal, who Himself lived it, must incarnate Himself within us by the Holy Spirit, that He may reproduce in and through us that which He has inspired us to desire. He must give us what He commands ; He must be in us what He prescribes.

# IV

# Silent Influence.

(MATT. v. 13–16.)

BEING is doing. Our greatest work for God and man is to be. The influence of a holy life is our greatest contribution to the salvation and blessing of the world. Though you cannot preach, or teach, or engage in some sphere of Christian service, do not be greatly moved, if only you can live the life of God amongst men. Our Lord for thirty years was content to live an absolutely holy life, as the Lamb of God without blemish and without spot; and His supreme work in the world was not only to give His life as a ransom, but to live His life that He might leave us an example, and that we should follow in His steps.

Too many Christians seem to suppose that the main object of life is to engage in a sphere of direct service, whilst they leave their personal character to take care of itself, and to develop almost at haphazard; whereas our main thought and care should be that Christ should be formed in us, and be revealed in every look and gesture, every word and act. Out of that will come naturally, inevitably, and blessedly, our direct Christian service. The best work is that which arises out of the simplicity and beauty of our witness for truth and love.

We must, of course, guard against extremes. On the one hand, we may attempt so much service as to neglect that inner culture which is priceless in its effect on service, and our personal inconsistencies will neutralize the effect of our Christian activities. On the other hand, we may sincerely believe that we are cultivating our character, when, in fact, we are sinking into a dreamy lethargy, from which we need to be aroused by the trumpet-call of duty to a dying world. We are apt to forget that the development of the inner life is not perfect, unless it issue in such going about doing good, as was the flower and fruit of our Saviour's thirty years.

.     .      .     .           .

*Though Persecuted.* Our Lord had been describing the reception which the type of character that He had come to implant would certainly encounter. Instead of attracting men by its heavenly beauty, it would certainly repel them. Instead of commendation and welcome, it would arouse dislike and rebuff. The great world of men would not appreciate the poor in spirit, the mourner, the meek, and merciful, the pure in heart, or the maker of peace—but would reproach, and persecute, and say all manner of evil falsely. But, notwithstanding all, He insisted that they should continue to bless the world by the silent and gracious influence of holy lives. Reviled, they must bless; persecuted, they must endure; defamed, they must entreat; threatened with death, they must still be as salt to their persecutors, and as light to their defamers.

However men receive our testimony, whatever they may say and do against us, notwithstanding the unreasonableness of their dislike, we must continue to be what our Lord would have us be; nay, we must *let* Him who is within us shine forth through us, so that men may be compelled to admit that the unearthly beauty of our lives is the supreme proof of the divinity and glory of our religion.

You ask what is the good of being good. Your detractors and oppressors vaunt themselves over you, take every advantage of your quiet, unresisting gentleness, and misinterpret your self-restraint.  It would almost appear that they are driven to greater extremes of wickedness, because of the provocation of your goodness.  The soldiers of the Roman governor probably never mocked one of their ordinary victims as they did the holy, unresisting Saviour. The gentle and loving wife will sometimes extract the most malignant and bitter hatred of her husband, such as he would show to no other.  But you do not know how your behaviour is beginning to thaw that iron-frozen soil, how often and deeply compunction is at work, or how nearly the hatred of your oppressor is being overcome by love.  The spring warmth may seem to fall on the frozen masses of snow and ice in vain, but every hour of sunshine is sapping the reign of the ice-king, and hastening the inevitable break-up of his supremacy.

That working-man who has borne the insults of his shopmates for Christ will presently have the ringleader come to beg his pardon, and with tears in his eyes ask him to pray for him.  That oppressed wife will have the pleasure of leading her penitent husband to the cross. That sister will be won by her sister, who has borne contumely and reproach with unswerving gentleness.  Be of good cheer, your sufferings will have their most blessed result in overcoming evil by good, as we have said. Remember, the Apostle speaks of "the kingdom and patience of Jesus," which means that patient suffering ultimately secures a blessed supremacy, a royalty, an overmastery of hardness and unkindness by gentleness, truth, and love.

When the Forth Bridge was in making, the workmen came to a crucial point, where one of the most important iron girders refused by some inches to come into position for the bolts to be driven through—a process which was absolutely essential to their union and the stability of the whole fabric. Every mechanical method to bring them together was tried to no purpose ; and finally, in despair, all further efforts were abandoned for the night. In the night a soft wind blew, and the sunshine of the following morning was so hot that the great masses of metal expanded beneath the genial rays, and, by the silent touch of the sun, the results were achieved which had defied the utmost efforts of force. So in human life, consistency of character, purity, gentleness, sweetness, such holy living as issues from the qualities which our Lord has enumerated, will avail when the keepers of the house shall tremble, and the strong men shall bow themselves.

.     .     .     .     .     .

The Lord knew well *the condition of the world.* To His holy and unerring judgment it was a carcase slowly rotting to putrefaction, and sorely needing some influence to stay its corruption. There was never an epoch in the world's history fuller of dazzling genius than that in which He was born. Some of the most brilliant names of history were shining still in the midnight sky when the bright and morning star arose over Bethlehem. But the grossness of the age was unparalleled and indescribable. The allusions made to it in the Epistles are sufficiently terrible, but the whole truth is only revealed in classic literature itself, which survives to show that the earth was corrupt before God, and that every imagination of the thoughts of man's heart was only evil continually.

In our Lord's eyes, also—to advert to the other metaphor —the world lay under the power of thick darkness. In its wisdom, it knew not God. Professing themselves wise, men had become fools. The god of this world had blinded the eyes of those who believed not, and they groped in the noontide as in the murky midnight. Such has been, is, and

will be, the condition of men without the Gospel. The
history of the human family is always repeating itself.
We cannot be surprised either at the description given, by
missionaries, of the awful condition of heathen countries, or
at the outbreaks of lawlessness and crime in nations which
are only nominally Christian. Our inventions, organiza-
tions, and boasted civilization, may affect the exterior of our
society, but if it were not for the presence of the Church
of the Lord Jesus, and the witness borne by the lives and
words of her members, there would be nothing to save it
from the pit of corruption, which has swallowed up every
great nation that has arisen to lead the race.

Men rage against "Exeter Hall," and revile what is
called "the Nonconformist Conscience," as they did against
the Puritans of bygone centuries, not realizing that they
evince the antagonism of corruption to the salt, and of
darkness to the light, and that the very existence of our
society is more largely due than they suppose to the very
elements they so much dislike.

*Salt.* Our consistent holy living will act as an antiseptic
to arrest the corruption around us. It is said that the
presence of a little child, with its blue-eyed simplicity and
purity, has often arrested the commission of dark crimes ;
and as much should be said of the influence of our own
daily living. A sudden silence should fall on certain kinds
of conversation when we enter the room. This or the other
form of worldly amusement, which has entered professedly
Christian homes, should be felt out of place when we are
staying there. And right through the society in which we
move there should be a consciousness that there is an
incongruity between our character and all that savours of
impurity, falsehood, or selfishness.

We do not want to impose a sense of restraint and gloom
on social gatherings when we enter. Our presence should

be an incentive to the merriment of the children, the cheer of the depressed, the gladness of young and old. Flowers should burst into beauty at our steps, songs should overflow in our paths, and innocent laughter should be our accompaniment. The mountains and the hills should break forth before us into singing, and all the trees of the field should clap their hands. Instead of the thorn should come up the fir-tree, and instead of the briar the myrtle-tree. But to all that is unseemly and unworthy our presence should act as an antiseptic.

A young boy, fresh from his mother's teaching and prayers, was plunged suddenly into a large lawyer's office, where he was articled. At first he was bewildered by his strange surroundings, then the crimson mantled his cheek, and tears brimmed in his eyes. "What's the matter with you, youngster?" said a coarse voice. "Do you want to go back to your mother's apron-strings?" "No," was the reply, "but we never said such things in my mother's home as you say here." The answer elicited a burst of laughter, but the head of the office said : "Gentlemen, this lad is right, and as long as he stays with us I must request that you modify your speech." And from that moment the whole tone of the office was altered. The lad's presence acted as salt.

We may easily lose our savour. Salt left in contact with a damp soil ceases to be salty, and is good for nothing but to be trodden under foot. It is neither fit for the ground nor the dunghill. Lot is an example of this. Sodom went on its way, regardless of his presence in its midst. The Seven Churches of Asia lost their savour, and, with those of Northern Africa, were trodden down by the Moslem. Nothing is so useless and worthless as an inconsistent and powerless Christian (Ezek. xv. 3–5). Oh, break your heart if sin is as shameless and reckless in your presence as in your absence! What have you done to forfeit the power you should exert? Repent, and do the first works! Yea, ask the Lord Jesus to infuse into you His own strong, sweet, pure nature, before whom the demons were driven forth, and by whose presence, through His Church in the world, an arrest has been placed on many of those grosser forms of sin which disgraced the society of His time, and still hold sway in countries where His name is not known.

What a comfort it is to know that our Shepherd restores the soul which is committed to His guardian care. If it turns aside into forbidden paths, or wanders in its own way, He goes after it, and brings it home on His shoulder, rejoicing. He will restore the years that the cankerworm and caterpillar have eaten. He can make Peter, in spite of his fall, a living witness to the truth, whom none of its enemies could gainsay or resist. It is His by His Spirit to infuse the old flavour into savourless salt.

# V

# Lighted to Shine.

### (MATT. v. 16.)

" NOT that Light." No, not even John the Baptist was that; there is only one true Light, "which lighteth every man that cometh into the world," even He who is the Life of men. We are lights; He is "that Light." We are stars that have no original glory, and if one differs from another in the radiance which he sheds forth, it is only in so far as he reflects more fully the lustre of that uncreated Sun. Centuries ago that Sun shone in this world, without a dimming cloud between His glory and the world of men, save the veil of His flesh; but so far as the world was concerned there was sunset, while it was yet noon, on Calvary; and we have been summoned to take up His mission and shine as stars in the midnight sky, or as candles in the darkened home, until the first beams of the eternal morning break on the Alpine summits of time, white with the snows of millenniums.

It is interesting to apply *the analogy between the Disciples of Christ and candles or lamps.* "The spirit of man is the candle of the Lord" (Prov. xx. 27). By nature we are like so many unlighted candles. As the candle is adapted to catch the light, but stands dark and cold until the wick is ignited, so have our natures been made to burn and shine with the nature of God, but they are unable to produce light of themselves, and remain cold and dark until kindled from the eternal Nature of Him who is Light, and in "whom is no darkness at all." It matters little what the

nature of the candlestick may be.  In your case it may be
of gold, silver, or china.  It may be exquisitely chased, or
of the commonest possible manufacture.  The most ornate
is incapable of producing the Light, and will be set aside in
favour of the commonest dip, stuck on the end of a piece of
wood, if only that has caught the precious Light of which
*the other* is destitute.  The Pharisees and Scribes of our
Lord's time were like handsome candelabra, which gave no
ray of light to the thick darkness of their age ; whilst His
disciples, humble fishermen, shone with a light which has
irradiated all succeeding time.

" *Men light a candle.*"  They place the wick against some
burning point of light, or they strike a match, or in our
days turn a switch ; and immediately there is a glow of
light which abashes darkness, and enables the housewife to
find her lost piece of silver.  O soul of man, have you been
lighted ?  Have you come in contact with Christ, or with
one of His servants in whom His nature has shone, or with
His Word, which may be compared to a box of lucifer
matches, because all its potentiality of fire and light
slumbers until called into requisition ?  If not, stand ex-
pectant and eager ; cry to Him, " Light me, O Light of
Life, and let my nature henceforth have no other purpose
than to shine on earth, as Thou shinest in the Eternal
Glory, emitting a radiance of the same nature and yielding
the same prism as Thine own."

" *The Life was the Light* " (John i. 4).  Notice those words.
Christ was the Light of men, not primarily because He
wrought miracles and spoke wonderful words, but because
He lived !  He was the Light of Nazareth, because He
lived within the circumference of its hills for thirty silent
years.  Galilee of the Gentiles—" the people which sat in
darkness "—saw a great Light, because " He came and
dwelt in Capernaum, which is by the sea."  The country of

the Jews was illumined, because "He went about doing
good, and healing all that were oppressed." The silent
influence of that Life, which unfolded itself in the loveliness of perfect deeds, has stolen over the world, like dawn
over the sky; and if the Lord had never spoken a word, the
testimony of His life, for God and Truth and Love, would
have been the most remarkable episode in human annals.
It must be so with us; we shine by what we are. We
shine as there is less of the wick of *our own* nature, and
more of the flame of *His*. We shine when we are unselfish,
when we "do all things without murmurings and disputings"; when we are "blameless and harmless, children
of God without blemish" (Phil. ii. 14, 15, R.V.). Though
you were never to speak a word, you might still fulfil the
greatest mission and ministry of your life, if only you
would live as Christ lived.

*"He was a burning and a shining light"* (John v. 35).
The Baptist shone because he burnt. His light cost him
life. On one occasion he said, "I must decrease"; and
probably his ministry lasted but a few months. The light
he gave was so brilliant that it exhausted him prematurely.
There can be no true shining without burning. The light
that costs you nothing is hardly worth the giving. You
ought to be burning down to the socket, as you spend and
are spent for others. Your zeal for God's house should
burn you up.

*Burning also stands for heat.* John was fervent, intense,
passionate, in his devotion. His was an ardent nature, that
loved as few men love. The love that others give to wife
and child and friend, in his case was expended on his Lord.
Mary did not more certainly break an alabaster box on the
head and feet of Jesus, than he the rich perfume of his
noble nature.

See that there is fervour, ardour, passion, the fire of a

burning heart, behind your testimony for the Saviour. Socrates gave light; he shone, but did not burn. Wesley gave light, but he burnt; and it is hardly possible to read a page of his sermons without being warmed at the fire of his intense nature. What shall we say of the Great Apostle, whose nature was ignited on the road to Damascus, and who said that whether he seemed beside himself or sober, he was mastered by one passion, and constrained by the love of Christ.

.    .    .    .    .

*The Bushel.* It would be absurd to take the trouble to light a lamp, and then obscure its rays by placing it beneath a corn-measure. The purpose of ignition would be counteracted and frustrated, if any inmate of the house were to cover the light. How many of God's children have placed bushels on the light of their daily testimony for God? The bushel of uncharitable speech! The bushel of peevish and murmuring complaint! The bushel of an unforgiving spirit! The bushel of some conspicuous failing! Any of these is sufficient to counteract the entire effect of our testimony. On one occasion, when a mother was remonstrating with her grown-up son for his not having become a Christian, he replied: "Mother, you have always seemed so afraid of God. Whenever anything has gone wrong in your life, you have been so put out, so fearful about the future, that you have made us think that we can get on as well without religion as with it." Is not this a specimen case of the bushels which cover our light? Whenever you hear men say, " He is a very good man, but —— ; " "She is a very good woman, only ——," you may be sure that there is some bushel in the life which is forbidding the outshining of the Life.

Notice what the Master says. "*Let* your light shine." It is not for you to ignite the flame, to supply the oil, or trim the wick; your simple duty is to guard against anything that may obstruct the outshining of the Life of God from your soul. If only you see to it that everything that might hinder the effect of your testimony and mar your influence is put away, Christ will see to it that your light shall effect the full measure of His Purpose. Permit those words to ring in your heart, "*Let* your light shine." Allow it to shine; guard against everything which would prevent it shining.

In contrast with the bushel is *the stand or candlestick*. Not under the bushel, but on the stand. What is your stand? Is it not your station in society, your position in the home, the sphere of your influence, your situation in some business-house, factory, or workshop?

With infinite care and forethought, God has chosen the very place in which you can do your best work for the world. You may be lonely, but you have no more right to complain than the lamp has, which has been placed in a niche to illumine a dark landing or a flight of dangerous stone steps. The Master of the house may have put you in a very small corner, and on a very humble stand; but it is enough if it be His blessed will. Some day He will pass by, and you shall light His steps as He goes forth to seek and save that which is lost; or you shall kindle some great light, that shall shine like a beacon over the storm-swept ocean. Thus the obscure Andrew was the means of igniting his brother Peter, when he brought him to Jesus.

What a good thing it is when a man takes his bushel off his light and turns it upside down, and places the light above it! Suppose, for instance, a man's bushel has been the love of strong drink. Let him conquer it, and put it under his feet; let him become an apostle of total abstinence; let him win other drink-cursed lives. Then that which had threatened to extinguish his influence will be the means of extending it, for others who have been cursed as he has been will naturally turn to him for help. It is a blessed thing when the fire of Divine Love kindles the bushels themselves, destroying them, and making a conflagration which compels men to turn from the power of darkness towards its attractive glow.

.     .     .     .     .     .

*The Motive.* Never forget that the one object in Holy Living is not to convince men, but to "glorify your Father which is in Heaven." If you live with your thoughts directed towards men, even though your motive be one of pure beneficence on their behalf, you will have less influence upon them than you will exert if your life be altogether Godward, and your one aim be that He may be glorified.

The glory of the Father was the one motive that occupied the mind of our Lord, from the hour when He said, "I must be about My Father's business," to that other when He stood under the shadow of His Cross, and said : "Father, glorify Thy name. . . . I have glorified Thee on the earth" (see also John xiv. 13; xv. 8). So live, speak, and love, that God may be glorified; and count your life a failure unless men turn from you to Him. It is not enough for your light to shine; it must *so* shine. Any shining which does not make men glorify God is deficient. Good it may be, but it is not the best. Your light must be so managed that men may not talk about *you*, but about *Him* who has made you what you are.

"Whether therefore ye eat, or drink, or whatsoever ye do, do all to the glory of God" (1 Cor. x. 31).

.     .     .     .     .     .

*God will supply the lamp with oil.* After all, we are but wicks, to the edge of which, as upon a ladder, the oil climbs

from the cistern. Who could see to read or work by the
burning of a wick? No; it is *the oil* that burns on the
wick, whilst the wick slowly chars, as it yields itself to
mediate between the fire on the one hand and the oil
on the other. Keep on burning, O Christian soul! God
will never fail thee, however long life may be, and however
dark the night! God will supply thee with the oil that
flows from the two olive-trees that set forth Christ's dual
work as Priest and King (Lev. xxiv. 1–4; Zech. iv. 1–3).

It is the constant fear of some Christian workers that
they will never hold out. But that should not be their
care. Christ ever lives, Christ ever loves, Christ is ever
and all sufficient. Draw upon Him; let all your fresh
springs be in Him; let Him be what God meant Him
to be—"wisdom, righteousness, sanctification, and redemption."

.     .     .     .     .     .

*God will certainly have to trim your light.* He will leave
this sacred business to no other hand than His own; and
He reserves for it "snuffers of gold" (1 Kings vii. 50).

Very often the soul dreads the application of His providence that seems to threaten it with extinguishment.
It turns out, however, that the love of God was only
cutting away something which was hindering our upright-
ness, that the true flame might break out more completely.
There may be limitation on the area of illumination, but
there will be marked increase in the intensity of the
radiance. The limitations of Paul's imprisonment meant
the lasting power of his Epistles. The snuffers of Bedford
Gaol produced the "Pilgrim's Progress."

Ask for a radiant life, and trust God to take the best
means possible in accomplishing an abundant answer to
your request.

# VI

# Christ the Completement of Human Life.

THE first question that an age asks of a new teacher is: "What is your relation to the past? What have you to say of the great prophets and teachers, at whose feet for generations our forefathers have sat?" To that question the reply has often been, "My mission is to destroy; you have been misled; the path by which former generations have travelled is by no means the easiest or best. I have come to suggest that we wipe the slate, that we obliterate the past, that we begin by laying new foundations on which to construct a larger and more commodious erection."

This is the creed of the revolutionary. In the French Revolution, Robespierre and his confederates went so far as to obliterate the septennial division of time, insisting that the week should consist of ten rather than seven days. New names were affixed to the days, to the streets, and to the officials of the State. But it was not thus that Christ inaugurated His work. He answered the *thoughts* of His age, saying: "Think not that I am come to destroy." Every "jot and tittle" of the ancient code was dear to Him. Jesus was no iconoclast. Radical though He was in going to the very roots of things, He was not a revolutionary.

As the noon fulfils the dawn, as summer fulfils the spring, as manhood fulfils childhood, as the great artist fulfils the struggling ideal of the generality of men in the poem, the statue, or the sonata, so does Jesus Christ gather up the highest ideals inspired by God's Spirit in men's hearts or engraven by His hand on tablets of stone. Wherever there is suggestion of eternal truth, He realizes it, and shows men the steps by which they may climb to its lofty level.

.       .       .       .       .

*Of course, there was a measure of destruction.* When the Epistle of the Hebrews was written, the institutions of the old covenant were becoming old, waxing aged, and were nigh unto vanishing away (Heb. viii. 13). But the destruction was only part of the natural process through which the ideal of the ancient Scriptures was being fulfilled. It was not a destruction which left no trace, as when the fire destroys the artist's studio, burning sketch and picture, the plaster cast and the finished statue—but the destruction of the imperfect form in contrast with the finished and completed design. Thus the rough sketch is superseded by the finished painting, the bud by the flower, the toys and the lesson-books of childhood by the interests of the mature man. The emblems of the kindergarten fulfil their work in the child's mind, by giving it conceptions of shape and form, and its first rudimentary knowledge. They are then cast aside; but the conceptions that they helped to form are the permanent possession of the nature, which thus made its first trials on the tiny lake, before it launched out upon the mighty ocean with its boundless horizon.

The Aaronic Priesthood was destroyed, that it might be fulfilled in the one unchangeable priesthood of the Son of God. The altars on which ten thousand victims had been consumed were destroyed, and their ashes poured out upon the ground, because they were fulfilled in that one Altar on which the supreme Propitiation was made. The Temple

was destroyed, because the Shekinah of God's Presence had
gone forth to fulfil that temple which is composed of saved
souls, and of which the Apostle says that "the building
fitly framed together groweth into a holy temple in the
Lord." The whole system of ceremonial observance, with
which Leviticus is full, has been destroyed, because love
has come to be the inner principle of the Christian heart,
and "Love is the fulfilling of the Law."

.  .  .  .  .  .

Under *the term* "*Law and Prophets*" our Lord includes,
by a familiar Jewish abbreviation, the entire range of the
Old Testament (Matt. vii. 12; xxii. 40; Luke xvi. 16;
xxiv. 44; Acts xiii. 15). It is probable that He never
possessed a copy of the Old Testament Scriptures for His
own private use. The only Bible that was within His reach
was that which was kept in the synagogue; but on His
retentive memory and heart as a child, Mary in the home,
and the old Rabbi in the school of the synagogue, and,
above all, the Spirit of Inspiration Himself, had deeply
written the whole text of Sacred Writ. It was thus that
He knew the Scriptures, though He had never learned in
the schools of the metropolis.

Nothing could exceed our Lord's reverence for the
Scriptures. He quotes or refers to them four hundred
times. With these He parried the temptations of the
wilderness; met and foiled the criticisms of Pharisee and
Scribe; and consoled His own heart when it was fainting
amid the shadows of Calvary. Everything that the
Psalmist had said of the law and testimonies of God was
literally appropriated by Jesus. They were sweet as honey
to His taste, "yea, sweeter than honey and the honey-
comb." In them He found the germ of the Messianic
ideal, which He realized in altogether unexpected ways,
and to fulfil which was His one eager purpose. It is not

without profound significance that we are told that on the
Cross He knew that "all things had been finished with the
exception of the one Scripture, which told how the rejected
hind of the morning" should be parched with thirst, and
receive at the hand of its foes not water but vinegar; then
"that the Scripture might be accomplished," He said, "I
thirst" (John xix. 28, R.V.).

From first to last the life of our Lord was the fulfilment,
in spirit and letter, of the ancient ritual. As the Son of
the Law, He obeyed the initial rite of Judaism on the
eighth day after birth, and there was no item of the law,
even to the dots of the *i's* or the crossing of the *t's* which
He omitted or slurred. "He died for our sins according
to the Scriptures, and He rose again the third day
according to the Scriptures." What could only be partially
true of His Apostle was literally true of the Lord: as
"touching the righteousness which is of the law, He was
found blameless."

Our Lord fulfilled the ceremonial law (Luke ii. 21, 22,
27; Gal. iv. 4), and fulfilled the moral law, since He was
Jesus Christ "the Righteous" (1 John ii. 1). He honoured
the law by His obedience "even to death," atoning for its
breach and violation by mankind, and giving, through His
unknown sufferings, an answer to its just dues and demands, such as could not have been afforded though the
whole race had been mulcted to the uttermost farthing of
penal consequences. His fulfilment, therefore, was not for
Himself alone, but as the second Adam, the representative
man, and for us all (Isa. xlii. 21).

.     .     .     .     .     .

"*The law made nothing perfect*" (Heb. vii. 19), because
it dealt so largely with particular instances and external
observances; and men sought to satisfy it by an obedience
which consisted almost wholly in "meats and drinks and

carnal ordinances," imposed until the time of reformation.
A servant in your home, who has been carefully trained,
may fulfil all the outward demands of household work; but
how different is the service which is compelled by an outward rule, and compensated for by the specified wage, from
the service which the wife and mother gives, inspired by a
love which feeds upon the sacrifices it makes! The law
could not produce perfect characters, because it did not as
yet deal with the principle of the self-life which vitiates
our best obedience. Indeed, the ancient ritual, in most
cases, even developed the self-principle, as in the case of
the Pharisees; because the accumulation of outward
obedience was deemed to produce a larger amount of
merit, and therefore to procure a higher place in the sight
of God.

Our Lord, on the other hand, came to teach that love
would fulfil all demands of the law and the prophets, *and
more*. He taught that to love one's neighbour would be
the fulfilment of the law, and that obedience to every Commandment was summed up in one word, "Thou shalt love."
In Christ's teaching the whole law was fulfilled in this one
word, "Thou shalt love" (Rom. xiii. 8–10; Gal. v. 14).

"Do we then make void the law through faith?" No;
since faith is capacity for God, it receives out of His fulness
the baptism of perfect love. More and more as we love we
establish the law (Rom. iii. 31). In proportion as we walk
after the Spirit of Love the requirement of the law is fulfilled in us (Rom. viii. 4). Thus Christ, in "shedding His
love abroad in our heart," becomes the "end of the law for
righteousness to all who believe;" and we present before
God a reverence for the ancient Scriptures, and a fulfilment
of their precepts, which could only be produced in us by
the Spirit of Love.

Is your soul enamoured with the love of some great ideal? And is it the complaint of your life that it has been too high for you to attain? Are you lying at the foot of the cliff, bruised and mangled by repeated failure? Are you almost in despair? Be of good cheer, Christ has come " not to destroy, but to fulfil," to take each yearning purpose and conduct it to maturity; to show how every desire for goodness may be realized, how the crescent of promise may become the full orb of fulfilment; and to accomplish in you and for you, here and hereafter, every " jot and tittle " of the Divine demands.

## VII.

# Love against. Anger.

### (MATT. v. 21-26.)

"THEY of old time," the philosophers and legislators
of mankind, saw that murderous anger strikes at
the very existence of the human family, and must
be arrested. They therefore prohibited it, and accompanied their prohibition by a threat of condemnation
before their high courts. "Whosoever shall kill," they
said, "shall be in danger of the judgment."

But neither prohibition nor threatening availed. The
dams they built were all too weak to resist the tides of
hatred and revenge that swept against their frail resistance. Men assented to their laws, that they were good.
In their saner moments, they acquiesced and assisted. But
when the storm arose within, they were swept headlong
from the thought to the wish, from the wish to the fully-
formed purpose, from purpose to word, and from word
to act.

Then the Love of God incarnate stood amongst men.
His legislation began further back, in the genesis of sin.
He does not deal with the act of murder, but sees, first,
the explosion of wrath in speech—*Fool;* then behind this
passes to the feeling of dislike—*Vain* fellow; and behind this
again the anger of the heart, concealed from all eyes but
His. In His judgment-chamber such anger is as evil as
murder is at the bar of man. He metes out to it the same
condemnation that human society allots to the murderer.

He says that every one who is angry with his brother is in danger of the judgment-court constituted to deal with murder. He does not say, "Thou shalt not kill;" because He deals with the springs of will, and thought, and action, creating a clean heart, renewing a right spirit, removing the evil disposition out of which murder springs. What need to tell a man that he must not kill his brother, when he has been led to love him as himself?

.     .     .     .     .

Our Lord refers to two tribunals of the Jewish commonwealth—the local magistrate's court, which had the power of life and death, and inflicted death by beheading; and the Sanhedrim, or final Court of Appeal, in Jerusalem, whose sentence of death was executed by stoning. There was a still more terrible fate than either, when the body of a criminal was cast forth as refuse into the Valley of Gehenna, here described as the "hell of fire," because fires were always burning in its forbidding precincts, to destroy the rubbish and garbage that would have poisoned the city's health. Where there is no system of drainage, as in Eastern cities, the pariah dog, the fire, and the worm, are indispensable.

In Christ's Kingdom, unwarrantable anger would be liable to the lower court, the anger that vented itself in slighting and contemptuous phrase to the higher, and the anger that exploded in vehement and passionate epithets to the fate of a castaway. He did not go beyond this, because the crime of murder would be impossible to those in whose hearts the first sparks had been judged and condemned. In the legislation of Christ, the man that hates his brother is a murderer, and any that allow hate to smoulder unchecked and unrepented of are guilty of a capital offence against His laws, and forfeit all the rights and privileges of His Kingdom, in the same way as murder

causes the murderer to forfeit all the rights and privileges
of the nation to which he belongs.

These are solemn words. They are quick and powerful,
and sharper than any two-edged sword. They pierce to
the dividing asunder of soul and spirit, and criticise the
thoughts and intents of the heart. They make us look up
at this humblest and meekest of men, speaking with such
authority, as He sets Himself above the level of those of
old time, with His majestic "I say unto you"; and lo!
His eyes are as a flame of fire!

Oh, soul of man, He looks into thee and through thee,
Art thou angry with thy brother with the heat of a selfish
and unjustifiable anger? Thou hast already been summoned to Christ's bar! Art thou cherishing bitter
contempt towards Him? Thou hast been already condemned to suffer the death of the blasphemer, for thou art
cursing one made in the image of God! Art thou flaming
with vehement wrath, like a burning furnace? Thou art
already in the hell of fire, it needs not that thou shouldest
wait for dissolution of soul and body. The flames of hell
have already fastened on thee. Thy sin is automatic in the
penal suffering it inflicts. Thus from our heart we come to
justify Christ, and realize that He is greater than the
greatest sons of the old time.

.    .    .    .    .    .    .

He goes deeper still, and shows how we may deal with
the first motions of our spirit against the ill-feeling which,
after long smouldering, breaks out into so great a holocaust.

So often we are angry with people whom we have
wronged; there is, therefore, no better way of saving us
from explosions of anger than by undoing the wrong, so
soon as we become conscious of it in the clear light of God's
presence. For this reason our Lord bids us find out the
brother whom we have wronged, and make amends.

Again, when we review the past hours in the twilight of any ordinary day, we often become aware that, though we have not allowed our ill-feeling to have its way, yet we have given some manifestation of it in a coldness of manner or change in behaviour which must have been noticed by our brother, our former friend, and have rankled deeply in his mind. The symptom of our altered feeling towards him may have been very slight, but quite sufficient to indicate, like the storm-signal on the coast, that there has been a depression in the atmosphere of our soul, and a storm is brewing. There is no more certain method of staying the progress of a tempest of anger, than by at once becoming reconciled to the brother over that one small detail in which our antagonism has revealed itself.

For each of these reasons, therefore, it is according to the deepest philosophy of the soul that our Lord bids us go to anyone who may justly have some cause of complaint against us, because of our manner, speech, or act.

.    .    .    .    .    .

*The altar*, of which the Master speaks, denotes some act of self-surrender to His adorable service which we are eager to make. Beside it stands the High Priest, waiting to consummate our gift, adding to it the merit of His inter-cession. The light of the Shekinah fire, which waits to consume the gift, is shining with intense brilliancy. All is prepared for the devout act of the soul which, constrained by the mercies of God, is about to present itself a holy, reasonable, and living sacrifice. Suddenly our great Mel-chizedek turns a searching light upon the hours which have recently passed. Every incident stands as clearly revealed as the objects in a landscape illumined by the lightning flash at midnight. And we hear His voice saying solemnly and searchingly, " Has thy brother aught against thee ? "

At first we shudder before the inquiry. We are conscious of some hidden wrong. The stiletto with which we struck at him was so sharp and slender that we assured ourselves against ourselves that the thrust must have escaped Christ's notice. But now we are aware that He, whose eyes carry the light with which they see, beheld it. We dare not deceive Him, but we evade His inquiry by enumerating the many causes of complaint that we have against the very person who has been the subject of our Lord's question.

" He has not treated me as I had every right to expect. He has been ungrateful, ungracious, intolerant. He has not considered my interests. He has taken advantage of my goodwill. I never can get on with him ; his temperament and mine are so different. Why didst Thou give him to me as my brother ? Had it been anyone else, we could have agreed. Outwardly I have tried to do my best. Canst Thou wonder that I hide a grudge in my heart, and that almost involuntarily it betrays its presence ? But, after all, the incident was a very slight one ; no doubt he has forgotten it before now. He is accustomed to give me ugly knocks ; probably his skin is too thick to feel so slight an evidence of my unfriendliness."

Again, the searching voice inquires : " Has thy brother aught against thee ? "

" It depends, O Master," we reply, " in what court the case is tried. In any human court, so slight a thing as that which stands revealed in this fierce light would be passed over as too trivial for notice. Before a jury of my friends, or even of my acquaintances, it would be admitted that I had not done anything so very wrong. It might be supposed that I was becoming morbid and introspective, were I to take action on such a triviality."

Again, that clear, strong voice is heard saying : " We

will not quibble. Thou knowest that thy brother is suffering, that he is losing faith in thy profession of religion,
that he is being prejudiced against Me ; thy parrying of
My question is thy condemnation. Thou knowest what
thou hast done. In excusing, thou accusest thyself. Leave
here thy gift at the altar. Go first, and be reconciled to
him. Then return ; I will await thee. Though hours may
pass, thou wilt find Me here."

"May I not offer my gift now, and then discover my
brother ? My heart is full of desire. I am eager to be
an entire burnt-offering to my God. Will not this fervour
pass away, and leave me chilled ? "

"Not so," the Master answers. "Thy present gift will
not be acceptable to God. The impetuous desire to make
it is of the flesh, not of the Spirit. If it were of the
Spirit, there would be no doubt about its ultimate per-
manence. To obey is better than sacrifice, and to hearken
than the fat of lambs. Be quick. The sky is darkening
with night. The road that remains to be traversed by thy
brother, who has now become thine adversary, is short.
Agree with him quickly, whilst thou art in the way ; lest
by delay the quarrel between thee and him becomes aggra-
vated, and thou find thyself in difficulties from which
extrication will be impossible. Every moment of delay in-
tensifies the sense of injustice, and makes more difficult thy
attempt at reconciliation."

"But he has wronged me, gracious Master. Is nothing
to be said to him ? "

"Not in the first place," is the reply. "It is necessary
that thou shouldest retract thy part, whatever it may be.
Ask his forgiveness for that ruffled feeling, that unkind and
harsh bearing, that icy reserve. Pay him any due that he
may rightfully claim. Ask his forgiveness as thou wouldst
ask God's, and thy approach will bring a flood of repentant

and protesting words, which will show that thou hast won thy brother. And if these do not follow, and he receives thine apology as his right, or without remark, still thou hast done thy part, and there is nought to be said against thee further. I will deal with him—then come, and offer thy gift."

What music then is in that word *Come!* All heaven speaks in the invitation. Come, says the Master, and render thyself a living sacrifice, which is thy reasonable service. Come, and let Me make of thee so much as is possible in thy brief life. Come, for all things are ready.

And we discover this—that when we have acted as love should act, not because we *feel* the love, but because the Master bids us, and we simply obey, then the Love of God bursts up in our heart like a hot geyser spring, and we find ourselves able to offer our gift to God with an emotion of love that we could never have experienced otherwise.

This is the glory of our Lord's teaching, that when we do what is right, altogether apart from the emotion of pleasure or desire, we find ourselves glad to do it. In the right act, there comes the right feeling; and in doing His will, we are able to say, "I rejoice to do Thy will, O my God."

Try it, O soul of man. Be indifferent to emotion. Act. The emotion will burst out like the flowers that carpet the meadows in May. The birds will sing, the streams will flow, the flowers will appear, because by one act the reign of the Frost King is broken.

# VIII.

## The Rule of the Eye.

### (MATT. v. 28.)

W E have already seen that if a man permits his heart to be filled with anger, that perpetually boils over or explodes in hard and contemptuous expressions, he is excluded from the Kingdom of Heaven, and cast away as useless—the fire of Gehenna being a well-known expression for the rubbish-heap. We are now led a step further, and taught that impurity may have the same terrible effect, unless its earliest motions be sternly repressed. Indeed, Christ teaches that whàt is as natural as a right hand or eye, may, unless rigorously ruled, become the cause of the whole body being cast into Gehenna.

The outward and inward, the expression by the body, and the passionate desire of the lower region of the soul (which we might call the animal soul), act and react on each other. The former influences the latter, as the pouring of oil arouses a smothered flame. On the other hand, through the combination of desire and imagination, contriving together in the dark caverns of the soul, the body may become the instrument of deeds that make the pure stars blush.

The legislators of the old time laid it down that no member of the commonwealth should commit adultery, and enacted terrible penalties if their prohibition were trampled under foot (Deut. xxii. 24); but the Divine Man, who reads the heart of man, goes back behind the deed to its premonitory stages, legislates about the look that may inflame passion; and condemns the soul that does not instantly turn the eye from that which allures it, to the All-Holy, asking to be cleansed, not with tears only, but with blood, and pleading that the eye henceforth may be filmed with pity, melted into tenderness, and set on fire with the light of *His* eyes, that are described as being like a flame of fire.

.    .    .    .    .    .

*The importance of the regimen of the eye* is acknowledged in many places of Scripture: "When the woman *saw* that the tree was good for food, and that it was a delight to the eyes"; . . . "Lot *saw* the plain of Sodom." It was to David's straying glances that his great sin was due (2 Sam. xi. 2). The Psalmist asks that his *eyes* may be turned away from beholding vanity. Job made a covenant with his *eyes*, and the Wise Man tells us not to *look* upon the wine when it is red, and giveth its colour in the cup. Each passage enforces our Lord's words.

.    .    .    .    .    .

The first step in the religious life is *to detect right and wrong*, not in the act, but in the thought and intention. If sin is arrested there, it is arrested in its earliest stage. When the inward senses are exercised, and trained to discern good and evil, and when the soul not only discerns but resists, there is no fear of the life being mastered by the tempter. The snake is killed in the egg; the microbe is destroyed before it can breed; the enemy is defeated before he can become ensconced within the city walls.

It is a remarkable fact to how small an extent many professing Christians practise this discernment between things that differ. They will be quite willing to admit that the soul has senses, duplicated with those of the body; that it has eyes, with which it may see God; ears, by which it may hear the inner voice; the sense of touch, and even of smell, by which to distinguish between the wholesome and the corrupt, between the air of Paradise and the breath of the pit. But they have never learned to exercise them, to note and act upon their earliest suggestion (Heb. v. 14). This is the cause of infinite failure, and keeps such Christians in the stage of babyhood. They never become full grown, nor partake of the solid food of the Word (compare also 1 Cor. iii. 1, 2).

A curious illustration of this happened to me once. A Christian lady was very anxious that I should read a certain novel, which had just come out and was attracting wide interest. She assured me that I should find much that I would approve of and enjoy. Acting on her advice, I took the book to beguile some leisure hours on the Atlantic, and sat down one afternoon on my deck-chair to enjoy it. When, however, I reached page 50, I flung it over into the ocean, as I thought its contents would injure the fishes less than myself. If I had continued to read that story, I should have been playing with fire.

What made the difference between that Christian lady and myself? Was it not that my inner senses were more sensitive than hers, and able to discern the evil of the book, which she would have unwittingly permitted to poison and contaminate her entire nature? Some of us have quicker natural senses than others. The coastguardsman, accustomed to survey the ocean, will detect a tiny boat which would escape the notice of the average landsman; the experienced eye of the scout will build up a whole volume of useful information from the examination of a footstep, or even a handful of ash, which would be of no service to the ordinary traveller. Similar differences hold in the realm of the soul; and many receive poison into their systems almost before they are aware.

It is therefore of the utmost importance to exercise the

soul in the discriminations of the inner sense, and to
accustom it to act on its findings ; and this was probably in
the mind of our Lord when He spoke so earnestly about the
rule of the eye, too accustomed to move carelessly over faces
and forms, on the spectacle of human and natural life, as it
passes in ceaseless panorama before us.   It would not have
been easy to speak to all the world about the senses of the
soul.   Men would not for the most part have understood
Him.   But if He could only teach them that there might
be sin in a look, and that the unregulated look might lead
to sin, it would be one step at least towards awakening the
soul to watchfulness against those first yieldings to temptation, which reveal themselves not only in the glance of the
eye, but in the inner movement of the soul.   Let a man
begin to guard his looks, he will end by keeping his heart
beyond all else that he keeps, since he has come to see that
out of it are the issues of life.

.    .    .    .    .    .    .

We must learn, most of all, to *conquer passionate desire.*
The appetites which God has implanted within us, for
food, for sleep, for human love, and such-like things, are
not in themselves wrong, but they are very liable to get
wrong in two directions.   Either we may desire a right
thing too passionately, and for the mere pleasure it affords,
rather than for the service it will enable us to do to others ;
or we may desire satisfaction from an object which, for good
reasons, is placed outside the circumference of our life.

The presence of such an object may excite the passionate
desire of our nature ; and, if it should, our Lord says we
must not look on it.   In this case, the old proverb, " Out of
sight, out of mind," is our only safeguard.   What the eye
does not see, the heart will be less likely to desire.

The Master goes further, and says that if we are brought
into almost constant contact with an object that tempts us,

and if we cannot conquer its inevitable fascination upon our temperament, it would be better for us to pluck it out and cast it away, though it were precious as an eye and useful as a foot. Of course, the best policy would be to acquire such an elevation and strength of soul that we should be superior to the temptation of any wrong or hurtful snare. When a child is well fed it will not fight with dogs for the garbage of the streets. When we come from standing on the Transfiguration Mount, with the light of its recent glory on our faces, we shall find no attractions in the vanities of Vanity Fair. But, failing that, and as the next best thing, it were wiser, like Joseph of old, to leave our garment and flee, refusing even to be in the same room with the temptress. At whatever cost, however, we must learn to master the desire of our senses, and not allow our feet to wander in the direction they solicit, unless it be one which God Himself has marked out for us. Even then we must tread in it with moderation, such as is imposed on the one side by the remembrance that every good and perfect gift is the Father's gift, and therefore to be used reverently ; and, on the other, by the fear lest we should injure another, and forget that in every act we must consider the well-being of all around us as paramount to our own enjoyment.

.      .      .      .      .      .

It must be, of course, always borne in mind that *sin is not to be imputed to the body*. It is not the eye that sins, but the heart that uses it for its sin. It is not the body that yields itself to the entrance of evil things, but the soul that turns the key, unlocks the door, and permits them to enter. No doubt the body is a weight in the heavenly race, because in its subtle nervous mechanism it carries the record and impulse of many acts of unrestrained evil on the part of our ancestors. It is a chain whose links have been forged by many separate acts, which have grown into habits. But the ultimate power is always invested in the spirit, which must always utter its *I will!* or its *I will not!* before an act can be done which has any moral quality in it, of which we must give an account, and which is either a step upward to heaven or downward to the pit.

If you sin, it is not your body that sins, but *you* through your body; and you are transforming into a pigsty what God made for His palace and temple. Strong as heredity may be, Christ is stronger. Vehement as the steeds are which are yoked to the chariot of life, the beneficent Creator would never have given them to you except that He knew that you were well able, with His grace helping you, to rein them in, and compel them to keep the course, and run the race, and win the goal. If then you want to arrest acts of sin in the body, it is imperative that you should deal with the inward sense and with the desires of the mind.

HOW THEN CAN WE PURIFY THE DESIRES OF THE MIND? (1) We must *guard against the first tiny thought of evil.* The microbes float in the air, and if at any time we are off our guard and allow them to alight, they will infallibly find a nest in which to breed. The Holy Spirit, if we entrust Him with the sacred task, will make us very sensitive when the tiniest speck of evil is floating toward us, and will remind us to shelter under the Blood. Men may shrink from our using that mystic word, but, believe me, there is no other infallible talisman of victory. "They overcame by *the Blood* of the Lamb."

(2) We must *avoid the occasions of temptations.* It is useless to ask God not to lead us into temptation, if we thrust ourselves thither. I had once to advise a young artist to give up painting figures, because it was impossible

for him to go through the training, which is held to be necessary, without being overmastered by temptations incident to that line of study. It was the right foot, but it always made him stumble, and it had to go. At another time I had no alternative but to advise a young girl to break away from an attachment dear to her as life, because she could not continue it without serious spiritual danger. It was the right eye, but it had to be plucked out. But are these losses without compensation? Nay, verily. It is impossible to give up such things for Christ, without receiving a hundredfold in this present life. When Milton's eyes were closed on the scenes of earth, they were opened on the Throne of God and the Lamb. We are completed in Him. We go maimed *into Life*!

(3) We must *appropriate the opposite grace*. It is good, but it is not enough to turn the eyes away from beholding vanity, or to shut them as the ascetic might do from all that is right and natural and innocent. There is something better, supplied by the universal principle, which we are using throughout these chapters—Love.

When our hearts are filled with love, the eyes will not gaze on an object for selfish enjoyment. They will look on the interests of another; will see all the agony and pain that may ensue if that other is turned away, as poor Bathsheba was, from the path of unsullied righteousness; will fill with tears at the very thought of bringing shame and dishonour into another's life; will become tender with a holy and selfless love; will be yielded as organs of Christ's own vision; and, out of all *that*, will come the transparency of a pure heart, which the Holy Spirit shall make His abiding-place.

"Who among us shall dwell in the everlasting burnings" of the Divine purity? He that "shutteth his eyes from looking upon evil, he shall dwell on high" (Isa. xxxiii. 14–16, R.V.).

# IX

# Simplicity in Speech.

### (MATT. V. 33-37.)

SPEECH! What is it? The vibration of the air set in motion by vocal chord, tongue, and lip. Apparently mechanical, yet how spiritual. Enriched from the voices of nature, the dash of the breaker, the murmur of the breeze, the song of the bird, and cry of beast, yet in its original fountains the evident gift of the Creator.

Speech is the utterance of the soul, and more, because the soul dyes and impregnates speech with its emotions and inspirations, so that they are communicated to others as by spiritual magnetism. Even when the words themselves are unintelligible, we catch the Divine afflatus, or our steps are quickened by the clarion appeal.

God spake, and the visible creation emerged from the realm of thought into realized fact. By speech the Law was promulgated from Sinai; and by speech He who spake as never man spake, and who was the Word of God incarnate, left us thoughts that can never die. Speech has burned with the vehemence of Demosthenes, flashed with the eloquence of Cicero, trembled with the pathos of Chrysostom, thundered with the emphasis of Luther, rung with the high note of Pitt, glittered with the brilliance of Sheridan, and poured like a torrent from the lips of Burke. What a wonderful gift is this of human speech. To what heights it may rise, to what depths descend. "Therewith bless we the Lord and Father, and therewith curse we men, which are made after the likeness of God. Out of the same fountain proceed sweet water and bitter."

The noblest form of speech is the reflection in simple and natural words of great and good thoughts which have been occupying the speaker's mind. Then language becomes strong in its simplicity, and majestic in its unadorned truth. There is small need for nicely-balanced sentences or highly-flavoured speech, when the soul of patriot, orator, or preacher, is aglow with exalted and inspiring conceptions. The volcanic fires that are burning within vent themselves in burning syllables, which plough their way into the hearts of men. When the speaker is deeply moved, his manuscript is crumpled in his hand, the precise words which he had carefully prepared are forgotten, and he makes a fresh way for himself in words that leap red-hot and alive from his lips. The yeas and nays of Christ have been sufficient to revolutionize the ages, not because of their eloquence (as judged by human standards), but because they are weighted with the wisdom and life of God. Terse, unadorned, and simple sentences—such, for instance, as Abraham Lincoln was wont to utter—are sufficient when far-reaching and profound principles of personal conduct or public policy have to be announced.

If, then, we would obey this command of our Lord as to speech, and confine ourselves to pure and simple language, we must begin to think more deeply, to love more tenderly, to cultivate our souls to nobler issues, and to amass spiritual treasure. We can safely leave our words to take care of themselves, if our inner life is pure, and sweet, and strong. Let us only imbibe our Master's spirit, and love God first and our neighbours as ourselves—then, from the pure fountain will flow pellucid streams like those that issue from the throne of God and of the Lamb.

.    .    .    .    .    .

It must, however, be sorrowfully confessed that for the most part the thinking of ourselves and of others is not

of that order.  Men are not true, or deep, or unselfish, in
their innermost hearts, and they know it; and therefore
in all ages they have endeavoured to atone for the poverty
of their thought by the extravagance of their language.

Men are not *true.*  To compensate, therefore, for their
lack of veracity, and to induce others to think that they
were neither lying nor deceiving, they have linked their
words with the awful name of God, daring the All-True to
step out of His silence and confound them, if it were not
as they said.

Men are not *profound.*  To compensate, therefore, for
their lack of deep and original thoughts, and to turn public attention from their threadbare and impoverished souls,
they employ extravagant and exaggerated speech, like that
with which a frivolous girl of the period is accustomed to
express herself when, for the first time, she stands in the
presence of the solemn majesty of the Alps, at flush of
dawn or under the touch of the silver moon.

Men are not *unselfish.*  To compensate, therefore, for
their conscious lack of that love which forgets itself in
its devotion to the interests of others, they will fill their
speech with extravagant expressions, which may impress
the ear and heart of those that hear them for the first
time, but fall vain and insipid on those who know that
the love which vaunts itself most passionately is more
than likely to be scheming for its personal advantage.

It is common enough for us to hide our nakedness, our
untruthfulness, our selfishness, under strong asseverations
and protestations, which call in the Supreme Being to
witness against us if it be not as we affirm.

.    .    .    .    .    .

The remarkable thing is that God keeps silent.  Though
His verdict be invoked by the habitual liar and blasphemer,
who swears that black is white, and calls on God to strike

him dead, or in some other way to prove that his words are false, yet Heaven makes no sign. No voice speaks out of the silence; no thunderbolt hurtles through the air; no sign is given that God is not mocked. Indeed, it might seem as though God had not heard, or that He was perfectly indifferent.

But such is not the case. There are many examples on record, like that, for instance, of Ananias and Sapphira, where, in answer to some blasphemous appeal, God has interposed to vindicate the truth which had been shamefully mis-stated. God is not indifferent. He is not careless of the interest of truth and righteousness. He hides Himself under the slow working of immutable laws. But He is never appealed to without sooner or later answering the appeal, vindicating innocence, and exposing the liar and the profane. With slow, silent, and inexorable precision, the Divine Government deals with all exaggerations, lies, and blasphemies, showing their hollowness, exposing their futility, and casting them up on the beach of the universe, to the derision of all pure and righteous souls.

In order to avoid using the Name of God in their protestations, men have introduced into their speech expressions which, in fact, derived all the significance they possessed from their association with Him. It has been a mean subterfuge. They have not liked to say, *By God*, or *By the Life of God*, and therefore they have substituted the phrase, *By Heaven*. They have scrupled to say, *May God strike me dead if I lie*, and therefore they have slightly modified their speech, and said, *By my life*, or *By my head*, though they know perfectly well that life and death are ultimately only at the disposal of the Almighty.

In our own speech we inherit some of these subterfuges, and apparently employ them without thought.

"*Zounds*," is a contraction of "By the wounds of Christ."

"*My dear*," or "*Dear me*," is an English form of the Italian, *Dia mia*, my goddess.

"*Good gracious*," or "*My gracious*," are clearly abbreviations of "My gracious God."

"*By Jove*," is, of course, the Latin name for Divinity.

"*Begad*," is "By God."

Many similar expressions will occur to the minds of my readers, and they all savour of the attempt to give the impression of solemnity and reliableness to our statements; and they have no other claim for consideration except that they are associated with the awful Name and Being of God.

   .      .      .      .      .      .

The Jews, like all Oriental nations, were especially given to these expletives, and sheltered themselves with the excuse that, so long as they did not mention the Divine Being, they might be excused. They said, "Thou shalt perform *to the Lord* thine oaths" meant that oaths which were not definitely made to the Lord, or by the invocation of the name of God, were not binding.

Our Lord shows the fallacy of this reasoning. He says that, whatever emphasis the allusions to Heaven, or Jerusalem, or the head, may give to our speech, is derived from their association with God; and that, therefore, if we would avoid the charge of blasphemy, we must cease to interlard our speech with such expressions. They are needless when our hearts are pure and our words sincere; they are objectionable, and worse, when introduced to give a false and unnatural emphasis to our speech.

As the disciples of Jesus, we must avoid, in dress, in expenditure, in our household equipment, whatever savours of extravagance. In all our behaviour, as well as in our speech, there must be the simplicity and beauty of Jesus.

Perhaps there is more truth than we would care to admit in the following minute of an old Friends' meeting : "It is the judgment of Friends that we should refrain from having fine tea-tables set with fine china, seeing it is more for sight than service, and it's advised that Friends should not have so much china or earthenware sett on their mantel-pieces or on their chests of drawers, but rather sett them in their closets until they have occasion to use them. And we desire an alteration in those things that Truth's testimony is gone out against, viz., the Friends' gowns made indecently, one part over long and the other too short, with lead in the sleeves, and that Friends should come to a stability and be satisfied in the shape and compas that Truth leads into without changing as the world changes, allso that Friends' cloaths may be of a decent modest colour, not hair cut or powdered, and neither coives to be made with gathers on the forehead, bordering on the fashion of the world."

This prohibition of our Lord, "Swear not at all," does not, in my judgment, touch on the subject of taking an oath in a court of law or on the assumption of high office. He is simply dealing with the use of expletives in ordinary speech. In His own trial, He did not scruple to be put upon His oath. When the High Priest said unto Him, "I adjure Thee by the living God, that Thou tell us whether Thou be the Christ, the Son of God," Jesus said, "Thou hast said."

And on one solemn occasion the Apostle Paul deliberately called God to witness that he spoke the truth in Christ, "his conscience bearing witness in the Holy Ghost."

It is not inadmissible that on occasions of high and solemn importance we should bare our heads as we stand before God, and solemnly ask Him to stand with us in attesting the truth of the words we speak and the vows we make. But there is a vast difference between this and the incessant and thoughtless appeal to God on every small and frivolous occasion.

. . . . . .

The true and holy soul finds God everywhere and in everything. Heaven above is God's throne; earth beneath, His footstool; Jerusalem, the holy city, the residence of the great King. Note these closing words—"the great King." We are reminded of the sublime words with which the last of the prophets rebuked the lax and slovenly worship of the chosen people: "From the rising of the sun even unto the going down of the same My Name is great among the Gentiles; and in every place incense is offered unto My Name, and a pure offering, for I am a great King, saith the Lord of hosts, and My Name is terrible among the Gentiles" (Mal. i. 11, 14).

Let us cultivate this thought, that God is not only our Father, but a great King, and with all the familiarity of little children will be mingled reverential awe. Wherever we go we shall recollect the presence of God, and this will prevent us from the spirit which is betrayed into extravagant speech. We shall not dream of using words which come within the scope of our Lord's condemnation, when we remember that every word is spoken in the presence of our Judge, and that of every idle word that we may speak we shall be called to give an account.

All harsh judgments of other people, who are God's creatures; all flippant reference to Scripture, to spice our conversation, and suggest witticisms and conundrums; all light remarks on God's dealings with men, as in a book once published, called "The Comic History of England"; all trifling with sacred subjects, or exposing them to ridicule—will be impossible to those who invest them with the thought that God is great, and greatly to be feared, and to be had in reverence by all that are about Him. The reverent use of the Day of God; the entrance with devout and sacred thoughts into His House; the wary and careful participation in the Lord's Supper; the loving handling of Scripture, and even of the Book which contains it; the honour with which parent and friend, old and young, are treated—all these admirable and beautiful traits, so necessary to the perfecting of character, are due to the same origin and source. When God is treated as the Great King, the whole life falls into symmetry and order, and becomes a prolonged *Yea* to truth, a profound *Nay* to falsehood and error, to the glory of Him who is God's Yea and Amen to all the needs of the human soul.

# X

# The Second Mile.

(MATT. V. 38–42.)

IT is the second mile that tests our character. About
the first there is no controversy. We must traverse it
whether we will or not.

Our Lord refers to the usage of the East in the trans-
mission of the royal messages. They are carried forward
by relays of messengers, much in the fashion of the Fiery
Cross in the Highlands, as Sir Walter Scott describes it in
" The Lady of the Lake." But the messengers were
pressed men, *i.e.*, each village or township was bound to
forward the message to the next, and the first man that
was happened on, however pressing his own business, was
obliged to afford the use of his horses or mules, and
go forward with the royal courier, giving him a mount and
accompanying him.

In the same way, emergencies are continually happening
to us all. We leave our homes in the morning not
expecting any demand for help or any other circumstance
to interfere with the regular routine of the day's engagements; and then, all suddenly and unexpectedly, there are
the sounds of horses' hoofs. A great demand has burst in
on our lives, and we are obliged to go off in a direction
which we never contemplated. We have no option. We
are compelled to go one mile, and then the question will
arise : Now you have performed what you were bound to
perform, and given what any other man would have given,

what are you going to do? The next mile is of prime necessity; it is in your option to go or not to go, and your action will determine whether or not you have entered into the inner heart of Christ, and are His disciple, not in word only but " in deed and in truth."

What as to the *left* cheek? That the right should have been struck is an incident which has happened to you altogether apart from your choice. It does not reveal your character in one way or the other, but your behaviour with respect to the left cheek will show immediately what you are.

What as to your *cloak*? Apparently your creditor can claim your tunic, and there is no merit in giving this up —anyone must have done as much; but when that is gone, what will you do about your cloak? This is the test of what you really are.

. . . . . .

But does our Lord mean that we should do literally as He says? Are we really to go the second mile, and turn the left cheek, and let our cloak go in the wake of our coat? These questions have been asked all along the ages, and answered as we answer them still. Each questioner must be fully persuaded in his own mind; and according to your faith, so it will be done unto you.

Many saintly souls have yielded a literal obedience to these precepts. It is recorded of the eccentric but devoted Billy Bray that in going down into the pit, shortly after his remarkable conversion, an old companion gave him a stinging blow on the cheek. " Take that," he said, " for turning Methodist." In former times such an insult would never have been attempted, for the whole country knew that Billy Bray was an inveterate pugilist. All the answer that he gave, however, was: " The Lord forgive thee, lad, as I do, and bring thee to a better mind; I'll pray for thee." Three or four days after his assailant came to him under the deepest conviction of sin, and asked his forgiveness.

The head of the constabulary in a great district in India told me that when he became a Christian he found it necessary to withdraw from the Gymkana (which is the European club and society rendezvous in most Indian cities), and his action in this matter aroused very strong feeling against him amongst his former associates. One day, as he was driving on the high road, a well-known society-man, driving past him in the other direction, rose up in his dog-cart and cut at him a tremendous blow with his whip, saying as he swore, "Take that, you . . . ." My friend, who is a very powerful man and of commanding presence, took it quietly, waited his opportunity of doing this man a kindness, and I believe it was the means of his conversion also.

In connection with a missionary society working among the tribes on the Congo, in which I am deeply interested, one of the missionaries resolved that he would teach a literal obedience to these words of our Lord, lest any evasion of them might lessen their authority over the hearts and lives of His people. His hearers were greatly interested and excited, and were not slow in putting the missionary to the test. On one memorable day they gathered around his house, and began asking for the articles which excited their cupidity, and which he had brought at such cost from home. In an hour or two his house was literally stripped, and his wife and he betook themselves to prayer, for, of course, it is impossible for Europeans to live in that climate without many accessories which are needless for the natives. But, in the evening, under the shadow of the night, one after another stole back bringing the article which he had taken away, and

confessing that it was impossible to retain it in his possession, because of the burden which had come upon his
heart.

Many such instances are probably occurring every day,
and compel us to believe that there is a range of laws
which should govern our dealings with our fellows, and
which are only unfolded to those who live not by sight
but by faith in the Son of God. Faith has been called the
sixth sense, and lays its hands on a third key-board of the
great organ of existence.

Far be it from us, therefore, to judge any who feel it to
be their duty to obey these words of the Master in all
literality.

.     .     .     .     .     .

But even if they are taken literally there must be some
reserves. For instance, when our Lord says, *Resist not
evil*, it is impossible to apply His words universally. Suppose, for instance, as we pass along a road, we encounter a
brutal man grossly maltreating a woman or a little child,
or a gang of roughs assaulting a fellow-traveller, it cannot
be that we are forbidden to resist the wrong-doer to the
utmost of our power. The whole machinery of the eternal
and invisible world is continually being called into requisition to succour us against "foul fiends," as Spencer puts it,
and surely we may do as much in these scenes of human
existence. Clearly our Lord only forbids us to strike for
purposes of private retaliation and revenge, we are not to
be avengers in our personal quarrels, we are to guard
against taking the law into our own hands, lest our passion
should drift us outside the warm zone of the love of
God.

It is the *personal* element in the resistance of wrong
that our Lord forbids; but He would surely never arrest
the soldier, policeman, or even the private citizen, from

stopping, so far as possible, deeds of wrong and acts of criminal assault. If thieves break into your home, or wicked men should try to injure wife or child; or if you should come on some poor Jew who is set on by robbers, who strip him of his property, and beat him almost to death, you are bound to interfere with a prayer to God that He would succour you.

And when the wrong has been done, as the Lord teaches us by His own behaviour, we may reprimand and remonstrate and appeal to the conscience and heart. When one of the officers of the court struck Jesus with his hand, Jesus answered him: "If I have spoken evil, bear witness of the evil; but if well, why smitest thou Me?" But there we must stop. We must not say in our heart: "I will be even with thee, and give thee as much as thou hast given me."

It is equally our duty, for the sake of others, to take measures to arrest and punish the wrong-doer. Supposing that a man has wronged you, and that you have good reason to believe that he is systematically wronging others; if you have an opportunity of having him punished, you are absolutely obliged, as it seems to me, to take such action against him as will make it impossible for him to pursue his career of depredation. If your lot should be cast in a mining-camp in the Far West, which was dominated by some swaggering ruffian, and he assaulted you, I do not think that you would be contravening the law of Christ if you were to give him so strong a handling that his power for evil would be arrested from that hour. It being clearly understood that you put out of your heart all private revenge and personal malice, and are living in a land where it is impossible to bring the wrong-doer before judge or jury, you may be compelled to act in a judicial capacity, doing for society what society is not able to do through lack of legalised officers and methods. Expostulation, argument, appeals to reason, might be employed first; but if these failed there would be necessity to use the only other argument that might be available.

It is clear, also, that we cannot literally obey the Lord's injunction to give to every one that asks. Else the world would become full of sturdy beggars, living on the hard-earned wages of the thrifty. And this would result in the undoing of society, and of the beggars themselves. Does God give to all who ask Him? Does He not often turn aside from the borrower? He knows what will hurt or help us; knows that to many an entreaty His kindest answer is a rebuff; knows that if He were to give us all we ask we should repent of having asked so soon as we awoke in the light of eternity. So when the drunkard or the drone asks me for money, I steadfastly refuse. It is even our duty not to give money indiscriminately, and without full acquaintance with the applicant and his circumstances, for we may be giving him the means of forging more tightly the fetters by which he is bound to his sins. A piece of bread is the most we may bestow upon the mendicant, until we have some knowledge of his character, his mode of life, and his real intentions. If only Christian people would resist the impulse to give money to beggars of all kinds, and reserve themselves for the more modest poor who suffer without making appeals, how much of the evil and sorrow of our time would be remedied!

.    .    .    .    .    .

What then does the Lord require of us? (1) *Do not take the law into your own hands.* In the old Mosaic legislation it was enacted that as a man had done, so it should be done to him. "Eye for eye, tooth for tooth"— "hand for hand, foot for foot, burning for burning, wound

for wound, stripe for stripe" (Exod. xxi. 24, 25). But in
the time of our Lord this had been interpreted as con-
ferring on a man the right to retaliation and revenge.
The Jews conveniently ignored Lev. xix. 17, 18, which
expressly forbade the private infliction of punishment.

When we are wronged, we must refer the wrong to the
great organized society of which we are part. Society will
lay its hand on the wrong-doer. The judge who sits on the
bench is not an individual, but the embodiment of society,
the representative of law and order; and if he condemn a
fellow-creature to penal servitude for life, there is no kind
of malice or vindictive feeling in his breast.

(2) *Turn retaliation into redemption.* When struck on
the cheek the instant impulse of the natural man is to
strike back on the cheek of the smiter. There must be a
second blow. But the Master says if there be a second
blow, let it fall on your other cheek. Instead of inflicting
it, suffer it. Instead of avenging yourself on the wrong-
doer, compel yourself to suffer a second blow, in the hope
that when you oppose your uncomplaining patience to his
brutality you may effect his redemption. The first blow
was of his malice, the second blow will be of your love,
and this will set new looms at work within his heart,
weaving the fabric of a new life. Thus the wrongs that
men have done to God led Him to present the other cheek
to them, when He sent them His only begotten Son, who,
when He was reviled, reviled not again; when He suffered,
He threatened not, but committed Himself to Him that
judgeth righteously. The patient sufferings of our Lord
have melted the hearts of men; and, as in His case, so in a
lesser extent it will be in ours.

(3) *Be large-hearted.* "Freely ye have received, freely
give." Do not be stingy and niggardly in your behaviour
towards men. You are obliged to yield the coat, give the

cloak; you are compelled to go for one mile at least, now, out of sincere desire to serve the purposes of the common-wealth, go another. The law compels you to give your cabman a shilling for two miles; but give him an extra sixpence, if he drives you to the extreme margin of that distance. The law compels you to pay your debts; but if you have incurred them, and they are rightfully due, pay them without haggling. There are certain duties in the home which fall to your lot to be performed: do them with a smile; *that is the second mile.* The husband must give the needed money to his wife for household expenditure: let him do it without grudging; *that is his second mile.* The employé must render certain services to his employer. If, however, he renders these reluctantly, doing only what he is paid to do, not entering into the spirit of his work, or doing it to the utmost of his power, he is like an impressed labourer, carrying the messages against his will; but as soon as he does his duty with alacrity and eagerness, even staying overtime to finish a piece of necessary service, *that is his second mile.*

(4) *Cultivate an ungrudging, generous spirit.* " God loveth a cheerful giver." Think of God in His incessant giving, Giving His sun and His rain; giving to the churl and the miser, the thankless and heartless, equally as to the loving and prayerful. That is to be our great model. We are to be stars, ever pouring our light on the vault of night; flowers, shedding fragrance, though on the desert air; fountains, though we rise in the lonely places of the earth, where only the wild things of nature come to drink. Always giving love and help to this thankless and needy world, because so sure that as we give, we shall get; as we break our barley loaves and small fishes, our hands will be filled, and filled again, out of the storehouses of God. " Freely ye have received, freely give." " With the same

measure that ye mete withal, it shall be measured to you again " (Luke vi. 38).

I want to add my testimony to the literal truth of these words. In my life I have found repeatedly that in proportion as I have given I have gotten, and that men have given into my bosom, according to heaven's own measure, pressed down, heaped up, and running over.

*For all this we need to have a new baptism of Love.* The love of God must be poured into our hearts by the Holy Spirit, who is given unto us. We must learn to unite ourselves with our Father's redemptive purpose, looking at the wrong done to us, not so much from our standpoint but from that of the wrong-doer, with an infinite pity for all the poisonous passion which is filling his heart, and an infinite desire to deliver and save him. One thought for his welfare will thus overmaster all desire for our personal revenge, and we shall heap on his head the hot coals of our love, to melt his heart and save him from himself.

# XI

# God's Primal Law.

### (Matt. v. 44.)

WHAT must be done for life—eternal life—the deepest and best? Everyone desires to know that. We all want to drink of the goblet of life, and to drink it to the last drop, to know everything that can be known in the brief limits of our existence, of true enjoyment. Everyone asks the question, in one form or another, How can I taste the inner meaning of life?

This is the answer—Love is life; and every man that loves perfectly God and his fellows is already drinking of the River of Water of Life, that flows from the throne of God and the Lamb.

You may be startled for a moment, having been wont to hear from the lips of teachers and preachers the formula, Believe and live. Is there then a contradiction when the Master says, Love and live? No, as you will discover so soon as you endeavour to live a life of perfect love without believing in Christ. You cannot do it. If you could, the Gospel would be needless; but because it is impossible for man to love like this, the Lord Jesus came to renew our natures and teach us to love; yea, He ascended on high to send the Holy Spirit, that He might shed abroad the love of God in our hearts. Love is not indigenous to the children of Adam's race; it must be implanted as an exotic from heavenly soil.

But when we speak of Love, we do not mean that it is primarily an emotion of the soul; it is the expression of

the soul in action. Love consists in being willing to do.
" Thou shalt love the Lord thy God *with all thy strength.*"
Many are disappointed because they try to love God with
their hearts, before they make Him first in their will.

How beautiful it is to see the amenities of human life—
the trust of man in his fellow, the love of parent to child,
the devotion of wife to husband. These things, like the
flowers that festoon unsightly ruins, adorn the lives and
characters and homes of men who lay no claim to godliness.
The abandoned woman presses her babe to her breast with
maternal pity ; the bandit is attached to his comrade, who
shares his rug and spoils and plunder ; and even the grim
tyrant is attached to the woman he calls wife. These
virtues are the wild flowers that grow over the rugged
nature of man. But they are not the test of our religious
life. If you simply love those who love you, and are kind
to those that are generous, and salute those who salute you,
you are not doing more than those who act at the prompt-
ing of their own human heart.

The children of God must do more than this. If the
religion of Jesus Christ does not lift its professors out of
the ordinary level of mankind, into an altogether new atmosphere, to stand amid a fresh environment, and to give
proof that they have found something which others do not
possess—it can boast nothing better than was yielded by the
hoary religions of the past, and is doomed to pass away.
No ; the Lord demands that, as there are men and women
in our social circles whom naturally we dislike, whose temperament offends us, and whose prosperity is a matter for
which naturally we cannot pray, so we cannot attain His
ideal until we have learnt to love, pray for, and bless them
with a Divine and heaven-born unselfishness.

How many Christians form a false estimate of themselves ! Their friends flatter them that they are generous

and kind, and with such estimates they are only too ready
to concur. We judge ourselves by the way in which we
behave to wife, child, or friend, to those in our own circles
of life, where it is easy to be open in heart and hand.
That, however, is far from being an adequate test of what
we really are. Men of the world can be attractive and
winsome under similar surroundings. The only adequate
gauge of the quality of our religious life is furnished by our
attitude towards those from whom we are separated by
prejudice, temper, or the consciousness of unfair and unkind behaviour. These relationships furnish the real test
of what we are before God; since we are towards God what
we are to them. Such an attitude of kindness and prayerful sympathy is impossible to men of the world. Thus
Christ's command is a profound and searching test, when
He reiterates the ancient law :

" THOU SHALT LOVE THY NEIGHBOUR."

(1) *Every man loves himself.* That is universally true.
The whole tendency and drift of human life, which has not
been regenerated by the Holy Spirit, is to revolve around
the pivot and centre of one's own individuality. This is
the result of being born of the first Adam, and proves the
necessity of being born again of the Holy Spirit.

(2) *Every man has a neighbour.* This is also taken for
granted. You are not only the centre of your own life,
but part of the circumference of someone else's life. That
circumference may be a very wide and far-extended one,
but you cannot evade the fact that you have been born
into a community or family of people ; and, as we shall see,
the point is not, who is your neighbour, so much as whom
you will neighbour. Any man whom you shall encounter
within the next hour on the king's highway, needing your
help, is your neighbour.

(3) *The world's method is at variance with God's.* The

children of this world try to limit as far as possible the number of their neighbours, and to admit as few as possible within the pale of their generosity; whereas God's principle is to go forth to all who need comfort and help The Scribes said, "Who is my neighbour?" (Luke x. 29), hoping that Christ would limit the duty of neighbourliness within as narrow limits as possible—a blood relation, or such like; whereas our Lord always taught that we were to be on the outlook to prove our neighbourliness. Go through the world exhibiting as widely as possible your neighbourliness. The Scribes said, "Who is my neighbour?" But the Lord answered, "Go, and show yourself a neighbour."

In showing ourselves neighbours, we must remember that every individual has

THREE CHARACTERISTIC PROPERTIES.

(1) *Every man has his rights.* There are his *inherited* rights, such as his right to freedom; for no man may enslave his fellow, and everyone in whose heart there is a part of God's love is bound, so far as he may, to secure liberty for the enslaved. Every man has a right also to fresh air, fresh water, sufficient land for the maintenance of life (whether cultivated by himself or by others is not material). Every man also has a right to freedom of conscience; so that no man is justified in imposing his creed or manner of Divine worship on another.

These are rights which every individual member of the human family has a claim to; and, if we would live a life of perfect love, we must respect these rights in every man, though a beggar; in every woman, though a servant-girl.

We all have *acquired* rights, such as those of character and of reputation. No one has a right to take another's character or impair his reputation. If there is some blemish in another's character which calls for reprehension and blame, dare to tell it him between himself and your-self ; but do not filch away his reputation.

There are also the rights of *property*. These must be respected. Anything like a *compulsory* division of pro-perty is impossible to Christ's disciples, though we all may proceed on the *voluntary* principle which was practised by the early Church, and of which the early chapters of the Acts tell so wonderful a story. Directly we begin to live the life of perfect love, we begin to respect the rights of another, and to care for them as if they were our own.

(2) *Every man has his necessities.* How infinite the variety of need ! The master needs the servant, quite as much as the servant the master. We are bound to each other by a network of necessities, and the man in whose heart is God's perfect love learns to minister to those needs, whatever they may be and whenever there is an opportunity—it being always remembered, of course, that a man may be compelled to turn aside from some needs he would like to meet, because of his duty to other and more clamant ones.

A recent writer has contrasted the demand of Christ with the demand of the world, as the contrast between ministry and mastery. The devil says : " Ye shall be as gods." Christ says : " Ye shall be perfect, as My Father is perfect." But, in order to be as gods, the devil says you must be prepared to trample men beneath your feet. Christ says : " If you would be perfect, go, sell what you have, and give to the poor, and you shall have treasure in heaven." The difference is that one set of men go bluster-ing over the world, showing the strength of their arm, and insisting on other men serving them ; whilst the other set are perpetually giving themselves away in ministry, losing their souls to find them.

(3) *Every man has his sins.* We often seem to forget
how clearly Christ has laid down our duty about our
behaviour to such. "If thy brother trespass against thee"
(Matt. xviii. 15), what do we do? We are cool to him, do
not speak to him, give him a wide berth. He has done us
a wrong, and we tell our wife and child to have no inter-
course with his wife and child. If we meet him in the
street, we bow stiffly and pass. But Jesus says, "Go and
tell him his fault between thee and him alone." Go? Let
him come to me. Go? Why should I? If he should be
in need or at the point of death, I would go, but why
should I go now? Yet the Lord will have us go, and
go now, that we may gain and win our brother to a better
mind. Ah, we shall never do it until we have learned to
love.

Yet another text, "If a man be overtaken in a fault, ye
which are spiritual, restore such an one" (Gal. vi. 1). Too
often we whisper to this and the other the story of his
sin, saying: "Of course you will not tell." But that is not
God's way. No, says the Lord; lovingly lift that fallen
man or woman up again in the spirit of meekness, remem-
bering how easily tempted you are, too. Then go to your
place of secret prayer, and pray God that you may not be
tempted to your undoing.

Once more: "If any man see his brother sin a sin which
is not unto death, he shall pray—— " (1 John v. 16).
Instead of talking of it, let us hasten away to a secret
place and cry to God. What will be the result? "God
shall give him life for those that sin not unto death."

# XII

# "Perfect as God."

### (MATT. v. 43–48.)

IN the garden the serpent suggested to our first parents that they should be as God, in knowing good and evil; but the Master tells us that we are to be as God, in the character and temper of our inner life. If His words here are compared with the parallel ones in Luke vi., we discover that He desires us to resemble our Heavenly Father, not in our knowledge—which would, of course, be impossible—but in our love and mercy. The perfection on which He insists is a perfection of love. Our natures are, of course, limited in extent and shallow in depth, as compared to the ocean fulness of the Infinite God; but a cup may be in its measure as brimming full as an ocean when the tide is high. Up to our measure we may become as full of Love as, in His far greater measure, our Father is; and this is what Christ demands, when He says: "Be ye therefore perfect, even as your Father which is in heaven is perfect."

.    .    .    .    .    .

This is the fifth illustration which He gives, that He is come, not to destroy, but to fulfil the law, by shedding abroad in our hearts that Love which is the fulfilling of that law; and it is interesting to notice exactly the change which He wrought in the ancient code.

The precept which our Lord quotes: "Thou shalt love thy neighbour and hate thine enemy," cannot be found in the Old Testament. On the contrary, its pages are strewn with the most moving exhortations to Love. If any of my readers would take the pains to investigate the matter, they would be startled to find the numerous exhortations to Love which are scattered through the ancient code—generally considered so rigorous and severe. "If," said Moses, "thou meet thine enemy's ox or his ass going astray, thou shalt surely bring it back to him again." And again : "If thou see the ass of him that hateth thee lying under his burden, wouldst thou forbear to help him? Thou shalt surely help with him" (Exod. xxiii. 4, 5). In a later age the same kindly spirit appears in the injunction of the preacher : "Rejoice not when thine enemy falleth, and let not thine heart be glad when he stumbleth, lest the Lord see it, and it displease Him." When, therefore, our Lord said : "Ye have heard that it hath been said, 'Love your neighbour and hate your enemy,'" He did not mean to refer to the inspired teachers of His people, but to those later Rabbis and Scribes who had overlaid the pure gold of Moses with their own incrustations.

There were two ways in which the teachers of the corrupt periods of Hebrew history had vitiated the scope of these ancient laws. First, they had obliterated the words, "as thyself;" and whittled down the precept from, "Thou shalt love thy neighbour *as thyself*," to "Thou shalt love thy neighbour." Next, they had, out of their own bad hearts, added the words, "*and hate thine enemy*"—lowering the Word of God to suit their own tradition.

Was it not high time that the moss and grit of centuries should be removed from the ancient characters which the Spirit of God had cut in the legislation of Sinai, and that Christ should re-edit the old law, doing away with the hateful additions, and enlarging the significance of that word "neighbour." They had delighted in limiting it. He rejoiced to level the walls of religious bigotry, jealousy, and national exclusivism, and taught that our neighbour is simply anyone to whom we can show kindness, so that the word stands for the universal brotherhood of man.

Our Lord desires that we should show love and kindness not only to man as man, but equally to our enemies as to our friends ; to those that curse, hate, and despitefully use us, as to those who will sacrifice everything on our behalf.

.      .      .      .      .      .

To enable us to realize such a command He suggests the Inspiration of a great Nature, a great Example, and a great Hope.

(1) We need the inspiration of *a great nature.* " Sons of your Father which is in Heaven " ; " Sons of the Highest " (Luke vi. 35). Men count much on ancestry. To be connected, however distantly, with the great of bygone times, is a subject of never-ceasing congratulation. To be able to point to some tomb, where the cross-legged effigy on the stone denotes the Knight Templar, or the shell indicates the pilgrim who crossed the seas on the Crusades, is of prouder boast than wealth and lands. To wear a coat-of-arms, which proves royal affinity—ah, how much is this ! And there is ground for it, because descent and blood undoubtedly count for something. When the special call comes there is something in heredity that answers it.

How much, then, must it not count for, when we stand face to face with urgent duty, that the capacity for its due discharge is certainly within us by virtue of our relationship to God through Jesus Christ ?

We have been born again by the Word and the Spirit. From the family of the first Adam, we have become grafted into the family of the Second. We are all the children of God by faith in Him, and if children then heirs, heirs of God, and joint-heirs with Christ. And because we are sons, God hath sent forth the Spirit of His Son into our hearts. Since, then, we are partakers of the Divine nature, we have within us the capacity for Divine Love. We may not be aware of its presence within us, but it is there, and if only we would dare to give it exercise, and allow it to make for itself an outlet in our kindly advances towards those who have served us ill, we should find that through the channels of outward expression the very fountains of Divine Love which are within us would pour their crystal tides.

You can love as God, not in quantity, but in quality, because God's own nature has been begotten in you, and awaits the opportunity of approving itself before men and angels.

(2) But we need, also, the inspiration of *a great example*. Who is there that has not sometimes stood on the mountain of Transfiguration, with Moses and Elias? A visit from some celestial nature, a biography, a noble act, a reunion which has revealed depths and emotion that surpass all previous experiences—these have greatly influenced our lives, and made us resolve that life should henceforth be new. And so our Lord brings us face to face with a marvellous illustration of the Love which He desires us to show.

Of course, He Himself, as He sat there, was the supreme instance of God's impartial Love. But the time had not arrived when He could speak plainly of Himself; so He selected His example from the humbler book of Nature, which He had often studied in His highland home, and which lies open before all men's eyes.

It was the month of April. Before His eyes was spread a charming landscape, on which probably the natural incidents to which he referred were at that moment taking place.

From its meridian throne the sun was shining. It was the Father's sun—"He maketh *His* sun to shine." It was *His* thought, *His* creation, the instrument of *His* benediction. "See," said the Master, "how the sun is shining on the children as they play their merry games, and at the same moment on the prison filled with hardened criminals; on the casement of the cottage, to revive the sick girl's drooping life, and on the path of the poor fallen one, as she avoids it, and steals into the shade; upon the little patch of ground belonging to the poor widow, which barely affords her a living, and the acres of the avaricious tyrant, who cares neither for God nor man, and would despoil her of her holding if he could. The sun shines equally on them all."

Then the Master may have pointed towards the heavy rain-cloud, born from the Mediterranean, which came trailing over the country, dropping its beneficent showers from its impartial buckets. Yonder lie two fields, with but a narrow fence between. That to the right belongs to an atheist of the worst type, who blasphemes God's name, underpays his servants, robs the widow, and browbeats the poor. That to the left is the holding of one who is as careful of his religious observances as the other is careless. The swift shadow of the cloud draws near. If it were steered by a human hand, it would probably be guided, so as to leave the one untouched whilst it poured its stores on the other. But there is no shade of difference in the distribution. The abundant and refreshing showers fall on either side of the fence.

.        .        .        .        .        .

Life is like an April day. It is not all sun, nor all cloud. The saddest lives have some patches of blue, some hours of sun. The happiest have some showers, and are overspread now and again with shadow. And surely this

is best, for those characters are not the noblest which are
spent always on the tableland, and never descend unto the
valley of shadow.    For *Sun*, you have had love at home, a
happy childhood, a loving wife, sweet children, prosperous
years in business, long spells of good health, happy episodes,
weeks and months of country or sea.    For *Rain*, you have
had seasons of ill-health, of business anxiety, and of
bereavement.    Now, if we were to compare experiences
between the men and women of our acquaintance in the
same position of life, putting away all considerations of the
inner peace of heart which religion gives, I do not suppose
that in the outward life there would be much apparent
difference.    There are thousands of homes where God's
name is not honoured—but where goodness and mercy, like
guardian angels, follow the inmates all the days of their lives.

Why?    Because the course of events in this world moves
by a blind machinery?    No.    Because God has no special
care whether a man be good or bad?    No.    But because
God loves His enemies, blesses those that curse Him, and
is kind to the unthankful and unloving.    If anything, He
seems more bountiful to those who oppose Him most, that
by His mercy He may lead them to repentance.

A man will sometimes speak thus: " I am one of the
luckiest fellows living; all my dreams have been realized;
I have a good wife, have not had an hour's illness, and
have never wanted for money."    Such men do not realize
that it is God who has given them all things richly to
enjoy, making no distinction between them and His dearest
children, because He longs to break in upon their shameful
neglect of His claims.    He gives " rain from heaven and
fruitful seasons, filling our hearts with good and gladness,"
that we may turn from vanity unto the living God, which
made heaven and earth, and the sea, and all things that are
therein (Acts xiv. 15–17).

We might, from the experience of these men, edit a new
edition of the parable of the Prodigal on this wise: that
when the father in the distant home heard that his son had
spent all that he had, instead of letting him come down to
the herding of pigs and the eating of their husks, he sent
him day by day supplies of sumptuous food, on each
hamper of which these words were inscribed, " I love thee
still; come home, haste to come home."

   .     .     .     .     .     .

But God has given us another and better *Sun* than that
which He has hung in heaven's porch. " He commendeth
His Love towards us, in that while we were yet sinners,
Christ died for us." And the benefits of the death of the
Redeemer are for the world. Therefore it was possible to
carry the Gospel, in the first instance, to Jerusalem. The
men who had used Him most despitefully lived there,
therefore the Master bade His disciples " to begin at
Jerusalem." " Tell Caiaphas, who sneered at My royalty
that I love him. Tell the grey-haired Annas, the irresolute
Pilate, and the mocking Herod, that I desire to bless them.
Go and find out the men who drove the nails into My
hands and laughed at My dying anguish, and say that I
will pray for them." So the Master left us an example,
that we should follow in His steps.

And God has given another and better *Rain* than that
which fertilizes the fields—the rain of the Holy Spirit's
influence and grace, which is for the most stubborn and
obdurate offenders. Did He not descend in copious
effusion upon the city of Jerusalem at the first, though it
had but lately crucified the world's Redeemer? Take
heart, you who think that you have grieved Him away, who
have done Him despite, who fear that you have committed
the unpardonable sin; even to you He comes with a shower
of grace, falling with refreshing bounty.

This is the example that we are to follow. Nothing less than God's even-handed love is to be our model. We are to be perfect, even as our Heavenly Father is perfect. We are called to be imitators of God, as dear children, walking in love, as Christ also hath loved us, even to the point of giving Himself for us (Eph. v. 1, 2). Anything short of this is not Christianity as our Lord taught it.

Dr. Abbott has said that he remembers, when he was a boy, sitting by the fireside of a little country inn in Maine, and hearing some men discuss the Sermon on the Mount. They were rough fellows, and one of them, scoffing at Christianity, said : " Thou shalt love thy neighbour— nonsense ! It is not in human nature." Exactly ; such love is not in human nature. Men love those who love them, and salute their brethren, and stop there. But it was in Christ's nature, and it is in the Divine nature ; and it is in the Divine nature to be imparted through Christ to those who claim it.

.    .    .    .    .    .

(3) We require, lastly, the inspiration of *a great Hope*. What animates a woman to spend her life on some brutal husband or ungrateful son ? Is it not the hope that, at last, her love will conquer ? And is it not this, in an infinitely higher sphere, that leads God, our Father, to pour out the ceaseless tides of His heart on the disobedient and rebellious ? Does He not see the consummation, when the heavens and the earth shall have become new as the result of His unstinted love ? And ought not the same purpose to animate us ?

It is recorded of a certain Chinese emperor that, on being apprised that his enemies had raised an insurrection in a distant province, he said to his officers : " Come, follow me, and we shall quickly destroy them." On his arrival the rebels submitted to him, and all expected that

he would take the most signal revenge.  Instead of this,
the captives were treated with the utmost humanity.
" How ! " cried his first Minister of State, " is this the
manner in which your promise is fulfilled ?  Your royal
word was given that your enemies should be destroyed,
and, lo, you have pardoned them all, and even some of
them have been caressed."   " I promised," said the
Emperor, generously, " to destroy my enemies.  I have
fulfilled my word ; for, see, they are enemies no longer ;
I have made friends of them."

We must henceforth amend our ways, lest we be counted
not worthy of Christ.  We must rise to the level of His
high demands, not in our own strength, but His.  And let
us remember two things : *First*, not to wait for an emotion,
but to obey by the sheer power of our will ; and, *second*,
to begin with individuals.

Have we an enemy who is always trying to curse us ?
We must be willing to bless him with the benediction of
our goodwill.

Is there someone in our life who envies and hates us ?
We must be willing to be kind and good, so long as we are
sure that our behaviour is not misinterpreted, or hurtful to
his independence and moral life.

Is there one who despitefully uses and persecutes us ?
We must compel ourselves to pray for him, until presently
a warm feeling of compassion fills our hearts.

Are there within our reach churlish and bearish people ?
Let us salute them, when we meet, with Christian courtesy
and grace.

Thus you will reach *perfection*.  It will not be the absolute and infinite perfection of God, for at the best it can
be only relative and finite.  It will not be the perfection

of angels, for they have never left their first estate. It will not be a perfection of knowledge, for we are all liable to error. It will not be freedom from temptation, or from such infirmities as weakness of body, dulness of understanding, and incoherence of thought. But it will be, after your measure, a full-orbed, equable, and loving nature, which shall go through the world shedding sunshine and rain on weary and hopeless souls, until they be led to take up heart and hope again.

A little child gets into a railway carriage. In perfect simplicity she begins to play with some austere-looking man, until he relaxes and the two become friends; and from them the genial warmth steals through the carriage, until everyone begins to talk kindly with his neighbour, and the tedium of the journey is relaxed. Oh, to go through the world like that, with God's radiance on our faces and His love in our hearts! Every day, be sunshine or rain to someone, and especially to your enemies, and the people from whom you are naturally repelled.

You say that all this is impossible for you. It is high: you cannot attain unto it. But remember those sweet old words: "When Israel was a child, then I loved him, and called my son out of Egypt. . . . *I taught Ephraim also to go*" (Hos. xi. 1–3). Ask your Heavenly Father to teach you to go; to put His Spirit within you as the fountain of His life and love; to work in you to will and to do of His good pleasure.

Everything lies in the will. Are you *willing* that His will should be done in and through you, in respect to the life of love of which we have been treating? If so, then yield yourself to Him, saying: "I cannot be perfect in love, unless Thou dost undertake to realize in me and through me the image of Thine own perfection."

# XIII

# "The Inwardness of True Religion."

### (MATT. vi. 1-18.)

IN the former paragraph of this wonderful sermon (vv. 17-48) our Lord began by laying down a general principle (v. 17), and then proceeded to illustrate it by five particular instances. First, He announced that His attitude towards the Mosaic institutions was not one of destruction, but of fulfilment; and then He showed that the love which He had brought to earth would realize all that Moses asked, and more.

The structure of the present paragraph is precisely similar, as appears from a study of the R.V., which substitutes for *Alms* (v 1, A.V.) the word *Righteousness*, so that the first verse is a general heading for all that follows. First, we have the general proposition that righteousness should not be done for the sake of display; and then we have that principle applied to alms, prayer, and fasting—the three departments into which the Jews divided their religious life.

That word "Take heed" is very searching. We are all liable to the temptation to put more and better goods in the window than we have anywhere else in the shop, and to show fairer samples than we can supply in bulk. Three times over in these paragraphs the Lord speaks of the hypocrites (vv. 2, 5, 16); and the hypocrite, as the Greek word intimates, is a stage-actor. We are all tempted to perform our religious duties for the show of them before others, and to appear in public arrayed in garments that we do not wear day by day. Our Lord called this spirit " the leaven

of the Pharisees," referring without doubt to the slight
and subtle beginnings of unreality, and its rapid growth,
filling the heart with fermentation and decay. Once you
begin to think that you must keep up appearances as a
religious man, and endeavour to do so; once you listen,
as Simon Stylites, to the murmur of applause which greets
you as above the average; once you assume the robes of
purity and piety to attract the gaze of your fellows—you
have admitted a principle into your heart which not only
will rob you of your reward in heaven, but will ultimately
eat out all the purity and loveliness of your religious life.

WE ARE ALL TEMPTED TO OUTWARDNESS IN RELIGION.
Some, of course, seek to acquire a reputation for piety to
serve as a cloak for their nefarious purposes. They weave
with assiduous care a rich vestment of alms, prayers, and
self-privations, to hide their unhallowed and self-indulgent
lives. Such people are, of course, mortified when any of
their religious acts do not come to the front and secure
notice. And when they have built up for themselves a
great reputation by their charitable deeds, they devour
widows' houses, and take a mean advantage of their wards.
Judas was one of these people; he had built up so great a
reputation that none of his fellow-disciples guessed that
he was about to do the deed of treachery. Beneath the
cover of his reputation he was able to filch the contents of
the bag.

There are others, again, who, with sincere and trans-
parent motives, began to love and serve God for Himself;
but as the days have passed they discover that they are
regarded as saints, and the sense of being held in reverence
by their fellows as " unco' guid " fascinates them. They
become as proud of their grace as others of their accom-
plishments or social position. They realize that they must

maintain their reputation at all costs.　Of course, the best way to maintain and increase such a reputation is to cease to think about it, and live only for the Lord Jesus; but directly we fail to do this, and occupy ourselves with our reputation and the long shadow it casts on the lawn, we are tempted to do things, not because God asks them of us, but to resuscitate our waning credit.　Our native character is getting a little threadbare, and instead of cleaving closer to God, we put a patch on the elbow or knee, by a generous gift, or a call to prayer, or the assumption in tone and manner of special sanctity.

(1) *As to alms*—The Jews were trained from their earliest days to be merciful and charitable.　The law of Moses continually inculcated remembrance of the stranger, the fatherless, and the widow.　Liberality to the poor was reckoned as part of religious duty towards God.　The prophets never forgot to urge the people to deal bread to the hungry, to bring the outcast home, and to cover the naked.　A row of alms-boxes stood in the Temple courts to receive the offerings of worshippers; and at every Sabbath morning service in the synagogues, appointed officers collected money for the poor of the town, which was distributed the same afternoon.　But in our Lord's time men gave their money to secure merit with God and admiration from men.　They bestowed their charity at the doors of the synagogues, where beggars congregated and passers-by could see; or distributed it as they came along the streets.

Mrs. Judson, in her account of the first Burman convert, says: "A few days ago, I was reading with him the Sermon on the Mount.　He was deeply impressed and unusually solemn.　'These words,' said he, 'take hold of my very heart.　They make me tremble.　Here God commands us to do everything in secret, and not to be seen of men. How unlike *our* religion this is! When Burmans make offerings at the pagodas, they make a great noise with trumpets and musical instruments, that others may see how good they are. But this religion makes *the mind* fear God.'"

Probably what has been said of Jews and Burmans is true of us all. It is apt to make a considerable difference to our gift whether the open plate is handed to us, and our coin lies open to all eyes, or whether the offering be gathered in a bag.

(2) *As to Prayer*—Our Lord, of course, is referring not to social, but private prayer. For the greater part of the day the doors of the synagogues stood open, as the doors of mosques or Roman Catholic churches do in foreign countries; and the Pharisees, at the three hours of prayer observed by all pious Jews, were not content with kneeling in the privacy of their own homes, but deliberately left their homes with the avowed intention and purpose of being seen in the place of public prayer. They took care, also, to be frequently overtaken in the streets, at the hour of prayer, that they might go through their tedious liturgies within view of all passers-by.

Amongst ourselves the tendency is certainly to conceal, rather than parade, our private prayers; and yet there is a subtle temptation to be more reverent in our demeanour, more careful in saying our prayers and reading our Bibles, when we are in the company of religious people, than when we are alone.

(3) *As to Fasting*—There were several fast-days in the Jewish year, in addition to the Great Day of Atonement, when the people were called upon to afflict their souls by public fasting. Yet this exercise did not always involve entire abstinence, but often consisted only in the sacrifice of a single meal. The Pharisees and others, however,

gave evidence of their exceptional piety by exceptional austerities, and took care to let it be known that they were fasting, by their gloomy countenances and squalid dress.

Our temptation is certainly not in the direction of fasting too much, but of never checking the indulgence of appetite in any degree or on any occasion. Probably we should be much healthier and stronger if now and again we were to reduce our meals and rest the organs of nutrition. But our temptation comes in another way. We affect a depression, a melancholy, a concern for our country, the state of our churches, the unorthodoxy of certain ministers, or a self-depreciation as miserable sinners, which we do not really feel. It gives us a certain character amongst our fellows, but it is hypocrisy in the sight of God.

There are those among us who never shed real tears of heartbroken grief before God for the state of things which they affect to deplore, but who pose among us as Jeremiahs. There are others who never catch a glimpse of real and pure fellowship with God, or of themselves, but they rush with it into print or speech; and whilst they are passing through such experiences they congratulate themselves that now, at length, they have something worth narrating in the experience meeting or the religious press.

This outwardness of religion is most injurious to us all. Plants subjected to sunlight by day and the electric light by night soon fade. What is the cure for it?

.    .    .    .    .    .

THE CURE FOR OUTWARDNESS IN RELIGION is the cultivation of a filial spirit. Our Lord lived the filial life to its perfection, and shows us what it is. Notice how all His thoughts seem to run up into the one absorbing central thought of the Father, "which is in Heaven." He is *thy* Father—His relationship to each soul is personal. He is

in secret, and is "thy Father, which seeth in secret," and
He waits "to reward openly." There is no need of vain
repetitions with Him, because He knows what we have
need of. All prayer is to be directed to Him. It is He
who forgives sins. It is He who clothes and feeds ravens,
lilies, and His children. From beginning to end, this
chapter is full of the Father, who was the One Spectator
and Audience before whom our Lord lived His earthly life.

Not only did our Lord paint the blessedness of that filial
life, but He came to give it to us all. This is what we are
called to know, and He has the power to make it ours.
Let us ask Him to do this great thing for us here and now.
"To them who receive Him He gives the privilege of
becoming sons of God, even to them that believe on His
Name"—"and because we are sons, God sends the Spirit
of His Son into our hearts." Then the Father finds the
child, and the child finds the Father; and such community
and closeness of intimacy ensue from this, finding that the
Father's smile and good pleasure become all the reward
that the child cares for. Oh, let us never be content until,
in our inner experience, God our Father becomes All in
all!

Then we shall never think of doing our righteousness
before men. We shall be good, not to win the approval of
our conscience; not because we are inspired by an abstract
love of virtue, as climbers may be ambitious to climb
some hitherto inaccessible peak; not even out of regard for
the welfare of others—but because we desire, above all
things, to give pleasure to the Father who is in secret.

Religion will thus become a sacred inward secret. We
shall have boldness to enter into the Holiest of All by the
blood of Jesus, and shall dwell in the secret place of the
Most High. Even when no earthly temple invites us, we
shall enter the temple of our own heart, and find God

waiting there, in those hidden depths which lie below consciousness. There we shall worship Him, who is a Spirit, in spirit and in truth.

To the Christian, it has been truly said, so far as any influence on his moral condition is concerned, privacy and publicity are words without meaning. He acts before men as he does alone, and acts alone as he does before men; for he is never "alone" from that one Spectator, who sees in secret, and whom he seeks to please. One presence fills, possesses, dominates him.

.      .      .      .      .      .

Do you know what this is? Since I have been forbidden to use my eyes for reading in a railway train, I have learnt some wonderful lessons in this direction. Sitting quietly in the carriage I have sought to unite myself with God, not asking Him to help me, but asking if I may help Him; not seeking His sanction on my schemes, but seeking that I may enter into His Redemptive purposes for those whom I love, for His Church and the poor hungry, needy world. It has been a fruitful experience, and I see how it is possible so to cultivate the sense of the presence of God, and the endeavour to know what is passing in His heart and thought, that one's absorbing impression tends to be of Him, and His will, and His good pleasure.

We must cultivate this openness of heart towards God. There must be no lie in our life, no lack of transparency or sincerity, no concealment or withholding. All the secrets of heart and life must be naked and bare before the eyes of Him with whom we have to do. We must watch against any attempt to seem more and better than we are. We must guard our life in secret as our most sacred jewel. And before we give, or pray, or fast, there must be the quiet gathering of the soul up before God, the silencing of every voice, the screening of all footlights and sidelights,

the descent into those deepest depths which no eagle's eye
has seen. Thus God's smile will become the supreme object
of our endeavour, as we admonish ourselves, saying : "My
soul, wait thou only upon God ; for my expectation is
from Him."

.    .    .    .    .    .

The manifestation of this inward fellowship will be
instantly and abundantly manifest. (1) *We shall realize the
Brotherhood of the Filial Life.* When we are near God we
shall begin to be occupied with the condition of His
children—our brethren and sisters ; we shall look upon
all our possessions as given us by Him in trust for them ;
we shall ask what He would have us expend on His behalf.
Alms-giving will at once become a sacred thing, into which
the stranger may not intrude—it will be entirely a matter
between the Father and His child. Even the left hand
will not know what the right hand gives.

Christian charity is not alms in the usual acceptation of
the term, but devoted service to the Father. Indeed,
Christ belittles the alms, and thinks only of the Father's
glory and pleasure. Alas ! that the Christian Church has
reversed this, magnifying the alms, and not stopping to
inquire the motive. What has been the result ? Millions
have been given, but the miseries of the world are no less.
We have pauperized and demoralized those whom, with the
best intentions, we meant to help. Before our alms can
really help men, we must get on our Lord's level. The
alms must be fed from love to God, as an inland lake is fed
from some secret burn, which pours into it waters from
mountains far away.

(2) *We shall become identified with the Father's Purposes.*
Our hearts are deeply wrought upon as we continue in this
blissful fellowship, until they pour themselves out in prayer.
"Ye people, pour out your heart before Him." But we

no longer pray for our way or plans. Instead of this we say: "Thou art holy and precious to me; I want to see Thee revered and loved; I desire that others shall see what I see; I find Thy will my heaven, and long to see all resistance and indifference brought to an end." Then daily bread, forgiveness, and deliverance from temptation, become so many means to the one common purpose and goal of our choice.

The soul that really gets quiet before God, realizing that He is in secret, is compelled to pray thus. You might as well stop the tide from flowing, birds from song, and children from laughter, as stop that soul from prayer.

> "Prayer is the Christian's vital breath,
> The Christian's native air."

(3) *We shall be full of Joy.* We may in our heart of hearts be laying aside this and the other weight, knowing that there is no merit in it, our only desire being to lessen the influence of the flesh, that we may promote the vigilance and clear vision of the spirit. It is entirely a matter between God and us, of which we breathe no word to others ; and when we meet our fellow-men, they will see a gladness on our face, and hear a ringing joy-note in our voice, that greatly commend the Gospel of our Lord.

Is there enough of this anointed head, and the face from which all marks of tears have been removed, in our modern Christian life ? How often we make no effort to be happy, or to make the best of things ! We have had a bad night, and have no scruple about imposing our miseries on a whole breakfast-tableful. We have a great anxiety gnawing at our heart, and we affect the appearance of bearing a heavy burden. I suppose there is in all of us a longing to be the object of our friends' solicitude ; and there are times when we may freely unburden ourselves to get advice and sympathy ; but we have no right to add unduly to the sorrows and anxieties of others, or to the travail of the world.

The life which is hid with Christ in God is a very radiant one, because it hands over all its burdens and anxieties to the Father in secret, and leaves them with Him. Thus it is "at leisure from itself," to enter into the anxieties of others.

What the future rewards may be of that inner life I do not care to speculate, and what the present rewards are words fail to tell. The reward of the hypocrite is the gaping wonder of spectators, who smile, criticise, and forget. The reward of the soul that lives with God in secret consists not in thrones or crowns of gold, but in a growing sense of nearness, of affinity, and of mutual understanding, which issue also in a growing likeness, though the saint wists not that his face shines.

## XIV.

# The Disciples' Prayer.

### (MATTHEW VI. 9–13.)

DEVOUT men, as their life unfolds, increasingly turn to prayer—not *prayers* in the plural, but *prayer* in the singular; therefore Psalm xc., which seems to register the mature experience of Moses, ends with the prayer : "Let Thy work appear unto Thy servants, and Thy glory unto their children. And let the beauty of the Lord our God be upon us." It was as though, after a long life of intense activity in which the Great Lawgiver had borne the people on his bosom as a nursing father, and when the activities of his life were drawing to a close, he was impelled to turn to prayer and catch up the yearnings, desires, and purpose of his life in one constant petition.

As we grow older, our prayers tend to become simpler and shorter, and more after the method of this prayer, which is so short, and yet so deep; so brief, that we may say it within three minutes; and yet so comprehensive and concise, that to be able to say it from the heart, and continually, is the very consummation and climax of the religious life.

*This prayer has been called the Lord's Prayer.* It might be more fitly known as the Disciples' Prayer, but it bears for evermore the Master's touch. It has been said that it was not original, and that these phrases had been on the lips of godly men in a former time. We cannot be surprised at that, because our Lord was always meditating upon the prayers of psalmists and prophets, appropriating them to His own needs, and weaving them into His own communion with the Father. But if the materials were furnished Him from ancient quarries, this prayer is the structure of His own thought; and as we tread its stately aisles, so severe in their simplicity, so majestic in their strength and far distances, we cannot but think of the myriads who have stood on the same pavement, been moulded by the same sentences and thoughts, and have found in these seven short but comprehensive petitions sufficient expression for their deepest, holiest moments.

Lonely sufferers and crowded congregations; little children just clasping their hands in prayer, and the saintly leaders of the Church; the Roman Catholic and the Protestant; the Anglican and the Nonconformist; the servant and his master—all their differences of creed or station, sex or nationality, are forgotten, as they enter to stand together within the precincts of this exquisite and noble structure. It is resonant with their voices, saturated with their tears, and ringing with their adorations. If, therefore, it may be called the Lord's Prayer, because He wove together the golden threads of olden time into the exquisite pattern which for symmetry and beauty cannot be surpassed, it may also be called the Disciples' Prayer, because in its use the whole Church has become one.

*Twice during our Lord's ministry He recited it.* In the first instance it was from the Mountain of Beatitudes in His manifesto to His disciples and the great world of men. On the second occasion He had been praying in a certain place, perhaps at early dawn. Whilst His disciples beheld Him rapt in devotion, they probably remained at a reverent distance; but when He ceased, they came to Him, and one, as spokesman for the rest, said: "Lord, teach us to pray." What a beautiful illustration of the power of unconscious

influence! Christ does not appear to have been constantly
insisting on the necessity of prayer, but He was constantly
praying Himself. His followers knew that in the early
morning He would depart into a solitary place for prayer;
and they could recall nights in which He had sent them to
their homes, while He climbed the mountain slopes to
be alone with God; and had they not seen the results, in
the transfiguring glory that stole upon His face, the com-
posure with which He passed through scenes of turmoil,
the power that demons owned? What wonder that they
desired to possess this sacred talisman of prayer! Happy
will it be for the Church and the world, when the glories
of true devotion will be so apparent, that men shall be
attracted by the evident gains of it to say: "Teach us also
to pray"!

These concise and beautiful petitions may therefore be used
*as a form of prayer*. In Luke the preface is, "When ye
pray, say." In Matthew the preface is, "After this manner,
or fashion, pray ye." It seems undoubted, then, that our Lord
meant His disciples to use these very words. "*When ye pray,
say.*" Crises often arise in our experience when we are
glad enough to know exactly what to say. It is a good
thing to have a mould into which to pour the molten metal
of fervent hearts. And sometimes, when the spirit of
prayer is burning low, the soul will catch fire at the
expressions used by those who have preceded it, and will
sweep up into the presence of God in horses and chariots
of fire. Forms of prayer may be used as aids to devotion,
but they must never become substitutes for the free out-
pouring of the soul.

But probably the loftiest use of this prayer is *as a model*.
It tells us the sort of petitions we ought to offer, and their fit
and fair proportion to each other. We learn that requests
for life's sustenance may fairly have a place in our daily

prayer; that we are perfectly right in talking freely to God about the recurring demands of food and clothes, about the common round, the daily task; though only one place in seven is to be given to these. Three are to be devoted to the needs of our inner life, and the rest are to be surrendered to adoration and intercession. Then again, we learn that our requests for ourselves should always be subordinate to those we make for the coming of the Kingdom, and the Hallowing of the Name. These come first in the prayer, and they should come always first in our thoughts and lives. This prayer, therefore, seems to be a kind of copy-book. At the head of each page there stands a petition in copperplate for us to go over, repeating it exactly; and below there is a blank sheet for us to fill in with petitions of our own, formed on the model of that at the head of the page, and yet as different as the Spirit of God and the exigencies of the moment may suggest.

.    .    .    .    .    .

We may obtain some general SUGGESTIONS FOR PRAYER. (1) *Prayer should be direct.* The Jewish proverb said, " Everyone who multiplies prayer is heard." They would babble forth a monotony of unmeaning sound, as the Mohammedans incessantly repeat, "Allah," and the Hindoos for days together repeat the monosyllable, "Om." And it was this senseless, unmeaning repetition of words which our Lord forbade. "Use not vain repetitions, as the heathen do." Let your petitions be simple, direct, intelligent. Say what is in your heart concisely, thought-fully, earnestly. Come to your Father as a child, and tell Him all your desires; and, having made your definite requests known, await the definite replies which He will certainly send. "Your Father which seeth in secret shall recompense thee."

Of course there are hours in all lives of Gethsemane

agony when the soul can only lie low and crushed before God, unable to formulate many petitions, and only able to repeat again and again feebly the name of Jesus, or the phrase He used so often in the hour of His own sorrow, "*Thy will be done.*" But this experience makes laws for itself. For the most part we must be careful not to pray by rote or by the hour-glass. A prayer which occupies, as this does, only three minutes to repeat, is prayer.

(2) *Prayer must be reverent.* Reverence is suggested by the words, "which art in heaven." Far be it from me to say a single word to discourage that holy familiarity with which the child of God approaches the Father. The tenderest words, the completest confidence, the closest intimacy, will be welcomed and reciprocated. But let it ever be remembered that the mercy-seat is a throne, and the Father a Great King. His abode is not only a home, but a palace, on whose floors angels tread with reverence, or, standing, veil their faces with their wings. Let us hesitate for a moment on the threshold of our prayers, and reverently unloose our shoes from off our feet. "God is in heaven, and thou upon earth; be not rash with thy mouth, and let not thine heart be hasty to utter anything before God."

(3) *Prayer must be unselfish.* "When ye pray," do not say I, me, mine; but *we, us, our*; not my Father, but *our* Father. Instead of teaching in abstract phrases the duty of intercession, the Lord so weaves it into the structure of this prayer that no man can use it without becoming a priest and pleading for his brethren. It is remarkable how, on the one hand, our Lord insists on lonely prayer: "Enter into thy closet and shut thy door, and pray to thy Father, who is in secret"; and yet a moment after He shows that that secret prayer is not to be selfish prayer, but linked with the needs of the great

family outside the chamber door. The prayer that does not recognise the needs of others as well as its own is not the loftiest prayer. A true appreciation of Fatherhood always involves the idea of Brotherhood. As Jesus said: I ascend to My Father, but He is also your Father; to My God, but He is also yours.

> For what are men better than sheep or goats,
> That nourish a blind life in their veins,
> If, knowing God, they lift not hands in prayer
> Both for themselves and those who call them friend?

In the moments of conviction of sin we feel to stand alone—no one has sinned as we; and we say: God be merciful to me, the sinner; I have sinned and perverted that which was right, and it profited me not. In hours of awful sorrow we feel to stand alone. Grief has a marvellous power of isolation—lover and friend stand afar off as we cry: "My God, my God, why hast thou forsaken me?" But in our normal experiences we realize that we are drops in a great ocean, members in one body, units in the multitude which no man can number, and who stand before the throne of Him that liveth for ever and ever, saying, "Our Father."

The door is always open; and, as you enter it, be sure to say, "*Our* Father," by which you include not simply your own brothers and sisters after the flesh—your mother and father, your wife and children, and the immediate relationships of your home—but a great company which is beyond estimation. The soul that can say "Father" is always conscious of being part of a vast brotherhood and sisterhood. Yonder is a woman who once lived to tempt, but now with a broken heart, in her poor, ill-furnished, dilapidated room, she is coming back to God, with words of penitence and contrition on her lips: is she included? Yes—"*our*." Yonder is a poor slave, whose flesh is quivering from the lash, and who, not noticed by man, is turning

in his despair to God: is he included? Yes—" our."
And yonder is a man who has always misunderstood and
suspected you, has put unkind constructions upon your
actions and words, and has imputed motives to you that
you altogether repudiate: is he included? Yes—" our."
Again, here is another whom you have been accustomed
to look upon as a heretic, because he does not exactly
pronounce your Shibboleth, though he holds the Deity and
saving work of our Lord: is he included? Yes—" our."

(4) *The true standpoint of prayer* is the honour and
glory of God. If we take away the invocation and
doxology, this prayer consists of seven petitions. The
first three concern God—the hallowing of His Name; the
coming of His Kingdom; the doing of His will. In this
our Lord Jesus could join with His disciples. Then comes
the single petition for daily bread. In this, again, our
Lord could join His voice with ours. Indeed, the whole
unfallen animal creation, and all holy beings throughout
the universe, may in their measure add their volume of
prayer that God would supply them with the sustenance
they need. But, in the last three, prayers are enumerated
for forgiveness, succour against temptation, and deliverance
from evil, which are only applicable for ourselves as fallen
creatures.

If you desire to pray aright, enter your room, where
God awaits you, kneel quietly before you attempt to
address Him, that you may realize His presence, and the
sights and scenes of earth cease to distract. Though it
may take many minutes before the silt drops to the bottom
and leaves the stream of your soul flowing pure and clear,
the waiting will not be lost time; it is only thus that the
blue heaven will be mirrored in the calm surface of your
soul. The next step is to unite yourself with God's mighty
purpose. Do not, in the first instance, ask what you want

for yourself. Compel the intruding crowd of daily need
and want to remain outside the fence with which you
surround the base of the mountain of prayer, and go up
alone to meet God, desiring to look at the needs of the
world and at your own little life as subordinate to all that
will make Him loved, honoured, and adored. Put God's
interests before your own. Enthrone God in your thoughts
and petitions. Put first things first. Go forth and stand
beneath the stars and count their number; mark their
mighty orbits; realize the immensity of the sweep of God's
movements—do this before you begin to count the glow-
worms at your foot, or the fireflies that glance around you
in the dark. On a campaign, the true soldier is more eager
for the safety of the whole army than he is mindful of his
personal need; his first thought is of that which will make
for his country's welfare; and he only puts in a plea for
himself that he may better serve the interests of his father-
land. At first, this seems to be an impossible ideal, but it
is, nevertheless, a true one; and we shall come to stand
upon this pinnacle, if we sincerely desire and intend that
our whole aim and purpose in this mortal life should be
to secure that God's Name shall be hallowed, His Kingdom
come, and His will be done. When we have poured out
our soul in petitions for these, we may begin to urge our
own need of daily bread and deliverance from evil.

"OUR FATHER." The suppliant must recognise that
there is a bond of nature between God and himself, such
as exists between parent and child. This has only to be
suggested for its importance to be recognised. A child
has a peculiar claim on its father. "You brought me into
existence; you gave me the nature I possess; you understand its movements, and yearnings, and instincts, by a
quick sympathy; you are bound by the strongest reasons
to give me that which you know I need. I am part of

you; and therefore lay claim that, as you nourish and cherish yourself, so you should nourish and cherish me." No stranger can introduce such tones into his speech. He may plead the claims of his need, of humanity, of gratitude, of friendship; but he cannot speak from the platform of a common nature. Amid a crowd of statesmen, state officials, court functionaries, attached and devoted friends, stands a young and slender boy; but there is a tie between him and the monarch, who is the centre of the glittering throng, which no other person, however noble, can claim; and his requests have, therefore, a deeper and more peremptory demand than those of others.

It is thus Jesus teaches us, that so we should pray. There must be an innerness, a filial confidence, an entrance into the heart of God, because He is your Father by adoption and grace. And whilst this must be your feeling towards Him, He will reciprocate it. Nay, He does not wait for you to approach Him thus; He anticipates your coming. As Judah said of Jacob, we may say of God: "His life is bound up in the lad's life." Like as a father pitieth His children, He pities us. He loves us not in a mass, but each alone. His family is not larger to Him than ours to us; and, as we have a niche for each individual child, so has God. We may refuse to trust Him, and to avail ourselves of His help, but we cannot alter those words of Jesus: "The Father Himself loveth you."

There are THREE CONDITIONS, in obedience to which we may realize that God is our Father. (Of course, there is only one Only-Begotten Son—One only that can spell His name with a capital *S*. All others are sons with a small *s*. There is an impassable gulf between the Divine Sonship and the human sonship, however high, and to whatever degree of nearness that sonship may be raised.)

(1) We all of us believe, with the heathen, that we have

*sprung from God.* This has been the cherished thought of man in every age and in every religion. The word Jupiter is made up of the two words *Zeus, pater,* the heavenly father; and travel where you may, under every sky, and amid men of every tongue, you will always find that this is their deepest thought—that there is an All-Father from whom man has sprung. But this is not the closest relationship; and it is not by this track that you will come home to abide most nearly to the Father's heart.

(2) Then, also, the Jews ever cherished the special belief that their nation stood in *a unique relationship* to God as Father. "Surely," they cried, in hours when anxiety and distress lay heavy upon their land, "surely Thou art our Father. "Though Abraham be ignorant of us, and Israel acknowledge us not, surely Thou art our Father." There was a kind of national relationship, therefore, between God and the Jews. But we cannot claim to stand with them on that ground, and the Lord Jesus showed that this sacred covenant relationship has been forfeited by their sin. "If," said He, "God were your Father," you would recognise Me—implying that they had no right to call God "Father," because they had broken the covenant tie. Therefore He came—and this is the very heart of religion—that He might, by the Holy Spirit, reproduce in the children His own nature and Spirit. It is only as we receive Him that we have the right to become sons of God, even as we believe in His Name (John i. 12).

(3) The Apostle says distinctly: "We are all sons of God *by faith* in Jesus Christ"; and because we are sons God hath sent the Spirit of His Son into our hearts, whereby we call Him Abba, Father. Moreover, in that remarkable Second Epistle of St. John the beloved Apostle says—and the words are very significant—"He that abideth in the

teaching "—that is, of the Gospel—" the same hath both the Father and the Son."

From all these and many similar references we may judge that, though we may belong to God as His offspring, we can never enter into the closest relationship until we are united by faith to His Son, who was born of a human mother, died on the Cross, and has now carried our nature to the right hand of God. By His Spirit we receive that nature into our own, and are thus in living affinity with the Son of God, who said : " I ascend to My Father and your Father, to My God and your God," as though He desired us to realize that by union with Him God became our Father in almost though not quite the same sense in which He was His own.

" HALLOWED BE THY NAME." The name of God is His nature—His attributes, the various properties that go to make Him what He is ; and when we ask that it should be hallowed, we ask that all which obscures the character of God should be swept away as mists before the rosy light of dawn. We thank God for all that is known of His wonderful being, for the message of Nature, for the revelations given to seers and prophets, for the life and death of the Son, for the gift of the Holy Spirit. But there are still great unexplored places. By reason of their sinful ignorance or superstition, men have misunderstood and misrepresented the character of God; therefore we pray that in this world, and in all other worlds, His glorious personality may be understood, appreciated, and loved.

" THY KINGDOM COME." In one of those sublime flights with which the Epistles of St. Paul abound, he tells us that the time is coming when the Son shall deliver up the kingdom to God, even the Father, when He shall have abolished all rule, and authority, and power. From this we are at liberty to infer that the kingdom was originally the

Father's ; that by man's sin and fall, it has been alienated from His control ; but that for purposes of recovery and re-demption, it has been handed over to the Well-Beloved Son.

The Lord Jesus became incarnate for the purpose of regaining the kingdom by His agony, blood, and tears ; though it is not as yet His, it is being acquired ; and it shall be His, and angel-voices shall ring out the glad announcement that "the kingdoms of this world have be-come the kingdoms of our God and of His Christ." When, therefore, we pray : "Father, Thy kingdom come," we are asking that the complete victory of Jesus Christ may be hastened ; that He may speedily triumph over all obstacles and enemies ; that all tyranny may be extinguished, all cor-ruption exposed ; that truth may reign in government, art, and science ; that trade may be free from chicanery and fraud ; and that He may speedily send forth His angels to gather out of His kingdom all things that offend, and them that do iniquity, destroying that last enemy, Death, and bringing in the golden age when all men shall know and love the Father, and become His obedient and loving children.

"THY WILL BE DONE, AS IN HEAVEN, SO ON EARTH." There is a close connection between the *Name* and the *Will*. The *Name* is the Being of the Father, the nature of God, what He is in Himself ; the sum total of His Divine attri-butes. The *Will* is the energy of God, going forth peren-nially and omnipotently to the accomplishment of His own Divine and loving purpose. Clearly, then, the will and the name are but two sides of the same infinite, holy, and loving Being, who is Love. Therefore, whenever we say : "Thy will be done," we should begin by saying, "Father" —"Our Father which art in heaven, *Thy* will be done, as in heaven, so on earth." It is because people catch up this petition suddenly, and without ascending to it through the regular gradients of the prayer, that it often seems so stern and terrible; but if only we can begin to say, "My Father," then add, " Our Father," and finally think of His nature, which, like some mighty ocean, full, deep, and placid, mirroring upon its surface the blue sky of eternity, is always sending forth tides of goodwill and peace in heaven and on earth, painting the tiniest flower that casts its shadow upon the lawn, and steering the mightiest world that rolls through space, always rising up in fountains of tenderness through heaven and earth—then we shall cease to utter this prayer as the address of the stoic, or the cry of the grieved heart, or the reluctant expression of resignation on the part of the suffering soul; and it will become the anthem, the psalm of the whole life. " Father, Father, in all worlds, in all ages, and in my little life, let the energy of Thy will work itself out to its fruition!"

But is not God's will always done, whether or no? Can any man resist it? Can any angel or demon overthrow it? Is it of use, is it wise, does it serve any purpose, to be ever saying "Thy will be done"? Surely it will be done, come what may. " He doeth what He will among the armies of heaven and the inhabitants of the world, and none can stay His hand and say, What doest Thou?" True; but are you quite sure that God's *best* will is always done? One is quite prepared to admit that generally, and on the whole, God's will is done, but is His best will done? The Royal will may be done, but is the Father's will done? And is not that the great difficulty in our world, that God's will is resisted, whilst something which is second or third best is substituted? The failure between God's best, and the best which becomes possible and practical because of our resist-ance, is that which brings discomfort, sorrow, friction, and pain, into our lives. But if from to-day we would say: " Heavenly Father, let Thy will be wrought perfectly," heaven would descend to brood in our breasts, and Paradise would come again to earth.

How many weary faces there are, tired and broken hearts, lives that have not fulfilled their full purpose and promise ! And is not this because, though God has been working upon them for many years, He has met with so much tough resistance and obstinacy that He has not been able to realize His cherished plan ? If only we would let the Father have His will with us, to what a height of blessedness, and peace, and strength, might we not come ! Young men and women, if, before you take the false and rash step—before you have allowed your own passions and desires to dictate your life-course—you would only let God mould you as tough iron in fire, what fitness there would be in that prayer : Let Thy will, the best will, the Father's will, be done, as it is done in heaven !

" GIVE US THIS DAY OUR DAILY BREAD." In the Greek language there are two words for bread—first, *cytos* (corn-bread). This, however, is not the word used by our Lord, but another, *artos*, which is a wider word, standing for food. It is as though our Lord knew that this prayer of His was to be world-wide in its use, and, therefore, selected a term which would cover equally the rice of the Hindu, the blubber of the Esquimaux, the macaroni of the Italian, and the oatmeal of the Scot—a general word standing for food. As He bids us to offer this prayer, several things are suggested.

These words suggest great rest of heart about daily supplies ; because, if Jesus Christ taught us to pray for daily bread, He implied that we had only to use the laws of prayer and labour, and God would supply all our need. He would never have put into our lips a prayer which was not in line with the thought and purpose of His Father. I know not what the anxieties of your life may be—about

your health, or investments, or situation—but I do assure
you that since Jesus Christ has put this prayer into your
lips, it is already a pledge on God's part that He will
feed you with food convenient, and supply the body with
all that it requires for its daily needs. "A body Thou
hast prepared for me"; and since Thou hast implanted its
daily-recurring appetites, Thou art surely responsible for
their necessary satisfaction.

It is possible, of course, to indicate many people—
perhaps God's children—who may be suffering from hunger
and privation. How is it that their food is so scanty and
inconstant? I reply: May there not be some lack in their
faith, and may it not be that they *have not* because they *ask
not*, or because they fail to exercise definite faith in God?

God loves to give, not bread alone, but fish. "They saw a
fire, and fish laid thereon, and bread"—not necessaries only,
but luxuries. There is many a pang of hunger in human
nature which remains when the physical deprivation and
want have been met. In fact, a good many would find it
comparatively easy to suffer physical hunger, if they were
delivered from suffering other unsatisfied appetites of the
nature, which are always crying out, "Give, give." For
instance, how many of us are hungering for *human love*,
sometimes to the point of absolute starvation, looking
eagerly for one tiny crumb to fall from a beloved hand, or
from the banquet on which others feast so bountifully?
Are there not some whose minds are voracious for *truth*?
They desire to understand mysteries that baffle; to pene-
trate the heavy mist that veils the eternal mountains.
Theirs is the spirit of John Foster, who would talk with
rapture of the revelations that waited on the other side of
death.

Besides these, are there not some whose deepest nature
cries out for God—for that Bread of Life that comes down

from heaven; for more of the indwelling and the nourishment of His character? These are they who have entered
into the meaning of the Saviour's own words: "Man shall
not live by bread alone, but by every word that proceedeth
out of the mouth of God." When, therefore, we kneel
before God in prayer and utter this petition, with some
the words mean: Give us to-day some gleams of human
love; some sign that our work is appreciated, and is telling
upon others for good; or truth upon which our minds may
feed and grow strong, for they that know God are strong
and do exploits; and, above all, feed our spirits with Thyself, for Thou hast implanted an appetite after the unseen
and eternal, which can never be met by anything which is
merely material and temporal.

When we say: "Give us, graciously and freely, bread for
to-day," do we not imply that all good and perfect gratification must come from God? Do you not like to emphasize
that word *give*? Do you not think that is a truer conception of life than that we must snatch at any gratification
which is within our reach? How often we are tempted to
make a raid on what promises to appease the yearnings of
our affection; to extract some word of appreciation; to
press into precincts where we have no right to stand, and
to ask for gifts from men which they have no right to
bestow. Yet, when we say this prayer from our hearts as
Jesus meant us to say it, we look up to God's face and
say: "Father, Thou madest our frame, Thou understandest
its appetites; Thou art well acquainted with all the
yearnings, hopes, and fears, that pass through our nature,
and I, Thy child, will take satisfaction from no hand but
Thine; give me what I really need for all the necessary
appetites of to-day." Then wait expectantly before God,
till there be some communication of Himself, some arrange-
ment of His providence, some sending of Titus, or the

advent of a letter, or telegram, or parcel, the glint of some new truth, or a text from the Bible, or a paragraph in a biography—something in which God shall Himself give us our daily bread.

Does your life seem almost intolerable in its penury, poverty, and precariousness of subsistence? Then turn to the Father and say: " I am determined to wait on Thee all day; not turning the stones into bread by any alienation of power or talent with which I am endued, but prepared to wait until Thou shalt open Thine hand and satisfy my need, or send Thine angels to minister." Surely God would never have placed within the scope of human nature any hunger, which is in itself natural and innocent, without pledging Himself at the same time to give it due nourishment and support! Besides, look into Nature. The birds of the forest seek food which has been stored for them in the berries of the autumn; the fish, as they flash from the lake, find the fly provided for them; the young lions, as they roar through the forest and seek their meat from God, find that He opens His hand and gives it. And it is impossible to suppose that He will starve those appetites which He has implanted. You may have to hunger a little, in order that more of the evil in the appetite may be eliminated, that its passion may die down, that what is wrong may be extracted; but the desire itself, in so far as it is part of the nature which He has given, will surely be gratified somehow, somewhen. Wait on the Lord, therefore, and be of good courage; no good thing will He withhold from them that walk uprightly.

No man has a right to utter that prayer unless he is prepared, so far as he can, to answer it. Obviously it demands that he should be prepared to work for his living; that he should go forth in the morning and toil through the hours of the busy day, coming back weary at night. It implies that he should put his shoulder to the wheel. It implies also, too, that he should not earn for himself alone, but for others ; and that, in so far as in him lies, he should minister to their hunger. A man has no right to pray thus who is not also prepared to untie his purse-strings, and, when there is really need for bread, to give it. But in a deeper sense the same thought holds true. We saw just now that hunger is possible for affection, for appreciation, for truth, for God ; and when we say : " Give *us* this day *our* daily bread," we really include all lonely hearts, all who weary for a smile, all who are pining for love, all who are seeking for truth, all who want God ; and, taking your stand amongst this ragged, eager, hungry crowd, you, as their spokesman, say : " Give all such their daily bread."

Does it not mean, also, that if you know some weary soul needing a kindly word you should speak it ? That, if you know of one who is famishing for human love, you should, if possible, pass some on ? That, if there are within your reach those who need the truth of God, and you can supply it, it should not be lacking ? That, if there are any who need that impulse of new vigour which comes from the touch of a spiritual man or woman, to reinvigorate, reani- mate, and reinspire, none of these should be wanting ?

Answer this prayer so far as you may ; and just because the world is so hungry, and weary, and famishing, go forth and be its bread-winners and its bread-givers. As far as you can, help to alleviate the despair and hopelessness, the misery and the sin of men, by passing on the Bread of God, the Bread of Life, the Bread of Love, the Bread of Hope, upon which you feed. Share your last crust with another. If you get a glint of light, flash it on. If you get a new truth, communicate it. If you get a baptism of the Holy Ghost, never rest until others rejoice in it too.

"AND FORGIVE US OUR DEBTS, AS WE FORGIVE OUR
DEBTORS." Every word in this prayer deserves our
thought. One might dwell at length on the conjunction
"*and*," for it is remarkable that by it this petition is con-
joined to that for daily bread; these only of all the petitions in this prayer are linked together. "Give us this
day our daily bread, *and* forgive us our debts, as we forgive
our debtors."

The conclusion is an obvious one—that we need forgiveness as often as we need our daily bread; that our need
for forgiveness is as urgent as our need for daily food; and
that the forgiveness of God is as lavish as His giving is,
which stores the cornfields with the golden grain, and
spreads so richly the repast of fruits and vegetables for
human need.

Do you recognise this? Are you conscious of this deep
need for forgiveness? Do you experience cravings for it
—insatiable as the cravings of hunger for food? Are you
aware that in God's sight your soul is starving, just because
you have not learned to know your own deep need? The
anodyne of worldly engagement has made you oblivious to
the hunger of your spirit; but if you truly knew yourself
you would never lift your heart to thank God for your
food without pleading for forgiveness; and there would be
the recurrent sense, that even in your happiest, holiest
days there are things that need to be forgiven, the blood
needs to be applied, the sense of God needs to mantle your
soul. "Give me daily bread—I want that; but as often as
I need it, grant forgiveness too."

The Greek word used by Luke, and translated *trespasses*,
means to *miss the mark*. Every one of us aims, as we hope
truly, at the mark; but we miss it, and we come back like
the prodigal, saying: "Father, I have missed the mark. I
meant to be a good and holy and dutiful son; I aimed at

it in my early life, but as the years have passed I have missed it."

But in Matthew our Lord sets forth another thought—that *sin is debt*, that it is a failure to pay our dues. If the one is the positive, this is the negative side. Trespass is positive, debt negative. " We have done the things we ought not," is trespass; " we have not done the things that we ought," is debt.

Every relationship means responsibility. Every tie by which we are bound to other men and women has its obligation, and there are times when the sense of our debts overwhelms us. Who is there of the holiest and best among us that is not sometimes absolutely overwhelmed by the sense of the obligations which have not been discharged, of the grievous debts which remain unpaid ? There is not a single man living who has ever perfectly discharged his debts to other souls, and certainly none who has discharged them to the Almighty. Warning bells are sometimes so constructed that they move with every movement of the waves; some are therefore perpetually tolling, every surge causes them to yield their monotonous note. Do you not realize that conscience is always tolling the bell of ought, of obligation, of dues not realized ?

Forgiveness in the old Anglo-Saxon is *forthgiving*. It is what you give forth ; what you give away ; what passes from your hand. The Greek word is to remit, to cancel, to dismiss—so that what has existed as an obligation ceases to be such. Our Lord then teaches us to ask that God would so remit what has been wrong, so cancel what has been left unpaid, that though in a sense we shall never be able to make right what is wrong to our fellows, yet the guilt of it will no longer accrue to us. When a man is truly forgiven, he may claim not only that the guilt will pass off his own soul, but that God's repairing hand will make right what has been left wrong; adjusting our undischarged obligations, so that those souls which have been wronged by us may, by His good hand, somehow be compensated. Sin is debt; but there is forgiving, remission, the putting absolutely away. The fact that our Lord taught us to use this prayer proves that we may count on an answer, because He was the Lamb slain before the foundation of the world, and He has taken away its sin.

When God says *forgiven*, He also says *restored*; and when the soul looks wistfully at those whom it has wronged, and says: " How about these ? " God seems to say : " I know the debt incurred; I have forgiven thee, and I will now repair." Then the blessed Spirit of God reaches out to the souls whom we have wronged; by a touch He transmutes the wrong, and into the wound pours the oil and balm. When a child of God understands that, his heart becomes very pitiful; having felt the agony of his own indebtedness and the joy of forgiveness, he begins to look around, and, instead of saying *me*, he says *our*. He thinks of his dear ones, and pleads, like Job, each morning, " Forgive the sins of my home." He thinks of the neighbourhood in which he dwells, and says: " O my God, I pray for these men and women around me, that Thou wouldst forgive them." Then, as a priest, he takes the whole world into his embrace and pleads : " O God, for the sake of Thy Son, forgive them; they know not what they do." The answer to that prayer is a Pentecost in which men are pricked to the heart, and led to cry for the mercy which God longs to show.

" THINE IS THE KINGDOM, THE POWER, AND THE GLORY." The authenticity and validity of this Doxology is questioned. Many ancient authorities, however, add it, and it does seem a natural termination for this glorious prayer. The Kingdom is God's, though His claims are set at

nought by men who say, Let us break His bands asunder
and cast away His cords from us. Yet God is King.

I never shall forget that archway in Damascus which for
centuries has looked down upon the misrule of the Turk,
but which bears the deep-cut inscription, " Thy Kingdom,
O Christ, is an everlasting Kingdom." Let us repeat it
again and again, " *Thine is the Kingdom.*"

" *Thine is the power.*" He has the power to set up His
Kingdom, to overcome evil with good, hate with love, and
darkness with light. Whatever ideals He may have raised
in the heart or for the world, to God belongeth power
enough to make them facts in experience.

" *Thine is the glory.*" This is the consummation of all.
We are told that in the campaign of the great Napoleon,
when his soldiers were being mown down in battle, they
would turn towards him waving their hands, and with
the last gasp of breath cry : " *Vive l'Empereur !* " So
in life and death we cry : " Glory to God in the highest."
This the climax of every prayer, the passion of life and
death.

. . . . . .

Our Lord returns to one clause in the prayer empha-
sizing the thought which was already implicated in the
structure of the fifth position, when He told us that in asking for forgiveness of our debts, we must always say : " As
we have forgiven our debtors." Notice the alteration made
in the Revised Version ; it is not " As we forgive," but
" As we *have* forgiven." This carries us back, of course, to
chap. v. 24, where we are told to leave our gift at the
altar, and to be reconciled to our brother before we offer
our gift.

Our Lord does not mean, however, that God's forgiveness is measured by our own, or that our forgiveness is the
cause of God's. Neither of these is the true rendering of

this clause ; but that God cannot forgive an unforgiving spirit.   The fact is that the only sure index that our contrition and penitence are genuine is that we forgive. If we do not forgive, if our heart does not go out in pity and forgiving love, it proves that we must have been mistaken about ourselves, and have never attained that true position of soul before God in which He is able to forgive.

Have you not noticed this in your own life, after the consciousness of forgiveness through the Blood of the Atonement (which is not mentioned here but implied), that the joy of forgiveness sometimes dies off your soul, and you question whether it was not a phantom, a bright and blessed dream ?   You wonder whether the words of absolution were really spoken, and wearily resume your burden. You cannot tell why it is, but it seems as though your sin had come back again on you.   Let me explain !   In our Lord's parable the king forgave the man who owed ten thousand talents, and the poor debtor was glad ; but leaving his presence he met a debtor of his own who owed him two hundred pence.   This man he took by the throat, saying : " Pay me what thou owest."   The result was that he was brought back to the king, and his pardon cancelled, so that he again stood liable for the ten thousand talents. Why ?   Because he was unforgiving, and the unforgiving man loses the sense of God's forgiveness.   The reason, then, why you have lost the sense of forgiveness is probably be- cause you have stood upon your rights, have insisted upon other men doing to you what you have failed to do to God, and because you have been deficient in the forgiveness that you have sought.   It is only when we have learnt to for- give that the Spirit of God maintains in our hearts the blessed consciousness of forgiveness.

How is it with you ?   Do you forgive ?   Or are there

men and women that you obdurately refuse to forgive?
If there are, it shows that your own soul is not right
before God; your love to God is gauged by your love to
men; your relationship to God is indicated by your relationship to your fellows. The man who does not love the
brother whom he has seen cannot love the God whom he
has not seen. Discover where you are to-day. If there
are men and women in your life that you refuse to pray
for and forgive, know that your heart is wrong with God.

Do the *first* thing, begin to pray for them, and say:
"Forgive *us*—that man who has hurt me, that man who has
wronged me; he needs forgiveness, but I need it equally.
We are both in the wrong; I might have made it easier
for him to do right than I have done." Begin with prayer.
That is the first step; compel yourself to pray " Forgive
us both." *Second*, ask for the opportunity to meet him.
*Third*, claim that when you meet there may be in you the
royalty of God's grace, that you may bear yourself with
that rare, gracious love which covers the multitude of sins.
Be willing that through your lips God's pitying mercy may
pass forth in words of human kindness.

May God, for the sake of Christ, cancel our indebtedness, and mercifully go over the wrongs of one's life done
to others and repair them! Then, if He gives us the
opportunity, may we use it to act justly, kindly, lovingly,
nobly, generously, towards those whom we have wronged!
" Forgive us our debts, and help us to forgive those that
are indebted to us!"

## XV.

# The Disciples' Use of Money.

### (MATT. vi. 19–24.)

THERE are two things which distort our eyesight—
*i.e.*, which hinder the pure intention of the soul:
the one is the temptation of the prosperous and
well-to-do; the other of the poor, reminding us of the seed
that was sown among the thorns. "This is he that heareth
the word, and the cares of this world (this is the temptation
of the poor and struggling), and the deceitfulness of riches
(this is the temptation of those who are endeavouring or
beginning to obtain property), choke the word, and it
becometh unfruitful."

It is of the temptations which accrue in dealing with
money that we have now to speak. Our message is to
those who, to use the words of the Apostle, *desire to be
rich.* These are they who "fall into temptation and a
snare, and into many foolish and hurtful lusts, which
drown men in destruction and perdition" (1 Tim. vi. 9).

．　　　．　　　．　　　．　　　．　　　．

Our Lord, first, alludes to *the ephemeral and destructible
character of earthly riches.* Oriental wealth consisted
largely of magnificently embroidered dresses; and in a
land where there were no banks (in our sense of the term)
coin would be buried in the earth—often, as in the case of
Achan, in a hole dug within the precincts of the house.
We are reminded also of the parable of our Lord about the
hidden treasure in the field, the owner of which had no

idea of the buried wealth that lay beneath the surface of the soil, until the ploughshare came into collision with it, and the metallic ring indicated that he should stay his oxen in order to disentomb the jar of coins, hidden when invasion swept the country, and which the proprietor never returned to claim.

Our Lord reminds His hearers that moth or rust will destroy all earthly treasures, and that thieves may at any moment break through the slight clay walls of their homes and carry off their hoarded stores. And surely His words are capable of an extended reference to that "crowned and sceptred thief," who shall one day dig through the clay walls of our mortal house, and take from us the raiment in which we have been attired, the wealth we may have amassed, the shares that stand in our name, the lands that we have purchased at such cost, sending us forth naked and despoiled, stripped of everything, into a world where we shall land as paupers, because we shall have failed to lay up treasure there.

Our Lord could not for a moment have *meant to denounce every kind of saving*. For instance, the Apostle Paul enjoins on parents the duty of laying up for their children (2 Cor. xii. 14). It is surely right for us to take advantage of the great laws of life insurance that we may make a reasonable and moderate provision against old age; and especially that we should, by a small annual payment, secure for those who may survive us an adequate competence. I seriously think that every young man and woman should, in the early years of their life, commence to pay into one of our large insurance offices, so that at the age of fifty-five, or sixty, a sum may be forthcoming which will be of use to them in their declining years—the same sum being paid to mother, wife, or sister, in case of their premature death; and I cannot for a moment believe that the spirit or letter of our Lord's words contradict this item of Christian economics.

It seems also certain that there is nothing in these words of the Master to prohibit the setting apart of a certain sum as capital, which may be used for the development of business, and therefore in the employment of a larger number of operatives. Nothing seems to me more beneficent than that a manufacturer should add to his capital, and therefore to his machinery and yearly output; for all this means the widening of his influence, and the provision of work to larger numbers of men, women, girls, and lads—the more especially if he contributes to the building up of some garden city, free from the facilities of drink, free from the confinement of the great town, free from the vices which are incident to every great aggregation of humanity, where every home is within sight of trees and flowers, where every working-man has his plot of land, and where the children breathe fresh health-giving air.

But neither of these methods of laying aside money is contrary to our Lord's injunction, "Treasure not treasures upon the earth." What He forbids is the amassing of money, not for the use we may make of it, nor for the securing of our loved ones from anxiety, but for its own sake, to such an extent as that the endeavour to hoard engrosses affections which ought to be fixed on nobler and diviner things, and leads to the concentration of the whole being upon the growing balance in the bank or the increase of Real Estate. In the judgment of eternity it is altogether unworthy of an immortal being to imperil his highest interests, his vision of God, his spiritual power, his peace and blessedness, for things which are so lightly held and easily lost as riches. Granted that the things for which men strive are no longer to be destroyed by moth and rust, or stolen by the night thief, yet the uncertainty of riches is proverbial; at any moment they may take to themselves wings and fly away. A panic on the Stock Exchange, depreciation in the value of securities, some new invention, the diversion of trade from one port to another, or the competition of the foreigner, may in a very brief space cause the carefully hoarded winnings of our lifetime to crumble and subside like the Venice Campanile.

. . . . . .

Our Lord might with good reason have denounced the practice of laying up treasure *because of the temptation which the desire to gain it involves.* When a young man enters life with the one intention of making a fortune as quickly as he can, he is almost sure to begin making it according to the maxims and practices which prevail in the world around him. From afar he sees the goal that beckons, and he is tempted to take the shortest cut to reach it, along a road strewn thick with lies and roguery, with lost reputations and blasted characters. That road is taken by myriads in the mad rush to become rich, irrespective of the misery which may be involved to others, and the injury which is being wrought for themselves. Well may our Lord describe riches as " the unrighteous mammon " (Luke xvi. 11). Therefore, with the utmost urgency one would reiterate to all who are commencing life, in the words with which the great Apostle to the Gentiles closed one of the last Epistles: "Charge them that are rich in this present world, that they be not high-minded, nor have their hope set on the uncertainty of riches, but on God, who giveth us richly all things to enjoy."

. . . . . .

Let us turn now to THE REASONS which our Lord adduces FOR HIS URGENT PROHIBITION against the amassing of treasure by His disciples.

. . . . . .

First, the hoarding of money *induces an inordinate love for it*. "Where thy treasure is, there will thy heart be also." There is a strong temptation to the most devout man who begins his life consecrated to God and to the best service of his fellows, when he sees money beginning to accumulate in his possession, to be attracted from the main object of life to his rising pile. Let young business men who bear the name of Christ test themselves, and ask whether their hearts are not being insensibly stolen away. They may not be aware of what is happening. Grey hairs are becoming plentifully strewn upon their heads without their knowing it. The fascination of money is one of the strongest in the whole world. It is almost impossible to handle it, whether it has come down as an inheritance from the past, or has been gained by successful trading in the present, without coming to like it for its own sake, to congratulate oneself when it increases, and to scheme for its further accumulation. Thus the heart becomes unconsciously bound by ever-tightening chains, as the balloon filled with the light gas, and meant to hold commerce with the clouds, is held down to the earth by strong hawsers from which it cannot get free.

It is not difficult for onlookers to discern the process by which the heart is being weaned away from the unseen and the eternal to the temporal and transient. There is a slackening of interest in religious worship and Christian service; an absorption amid the home-circle which shows that the heart is no longer there ; a reluctance to part with money that used once to be freely given for home and foreign missions. It becomes increasingly difficult to engage the attention in anything which involves the diversion of time or thought from the bank, the factory, or the store. The process is very subtle; but, on the comparison of years, those who love the tempted and fascinated nature, shake their heads gravely as they realize that the heart is being betrayed to its ruin, and that another life will soon be cast beneath the wheels of the terrible Juggernaut Car of worldly ambition and success.

There are five tests by which we may become aware whether this parasite is wrapping itself around us. Let us dare to question our hearts, and ask God to search them by His Holy Spirit. These five will suffice:—

(1) Do we find our mind going towards the little store of money which we have made, with a considerable amount of complacency, casting up again and again its amount, and calculating how much more may be added in the course of another year? When we are sleepless at night, or sit back in the corner of our railway carriage, do we find ourselves habitually going in the one direction of that growing competence? If so, is it not clear that our heart is being fascinated and attracted?

(2) Does the thought constantly intrude in our mind that there is now less likelihood than ever of our spending the end of our days in a respectable workhouse, or being dependent upon others, even upon God Himself? Do we look back upon the days of early manhood and compare them with the present, feeling that we are becoming independent? Is our trust in God less complete than it used to be? Is there not danger, therefore, of our weak and deceitful heart trusting in these uncertain riches, and being robbed of that simple faith which used to be the charm of earlier days, when we were content to do His work and trust Him for all that was necessary?

(3) Do we envy other men who are making money more rapidly than we are, and count ourselves ill-used if we cannot keep pace with them?

(4) Do we look at every service we perform—at our extending knowledge of men, at every new piece of

information that we gather—in the light of their monetary advantage?

(5) Is it our habit to measure the gains of the year simply by what we have made, and with no reference to what we are, to the money we have accumulated, rather than the good we have done?

It becomes us to ask ourselves such questions as these reverently, as in the sight of God, and thoughtfully for our own highest interests; for they will reveal to us almost certainly whether the slow poison of an absorbing love of money may not be stealing through our heart, robbing it of its noblest attributes. It is a terrible thing for us to love gold for its own sake, rather than for the use that we may make of it, because the heart is liable to become like that which it loves. Not only is the heart buried in the place where the treasure is, but inevitably it becomes like its treasure. Ossification is a terrible physical disease, when the heart turns to a hard, bony substance; but it has a spiritual counterpart for those beneath whose love for gold the heart shrivels into something little better than metal.

.    .    .    .    .    .

It is not necessary for us to dwell at length on the second reason which our Lord adduces against treasuring our treasures, viz., that hoarding money *diverts the pure intention of the soul and blinds all spiritual light.* We all know that faith is only possible for the pure heart. The faculty of spiritual vision and receptivity depends upon the simplicity and integrity of our moral life. When, therefore, the heart is filled with thoughts of its earthly riches, it becomes gross and insensible to the spiritual and eternal realm. Things of God fade from the vision, the love of God declines from the heart, the soul is no longer single in its purpose, the eye becomes dim, the spiritual force abated, moral paralysis sets in, and the whole body becomes full of darkness, under the cover of which evil things creep forth. Oh, do not let your spiritual eyes become dazzled by the glitter of this world's goods, lest you be unable, like Bunyan's man with the muck-rake, to see the angel who, with golden crown in hand, waits to bless you. Instead of crouching over the heap of transient treasure, rise to your full stature, and claim the crown that fadeth not away!

.    .    .    .    .    .

The third reason that our Lord adduces is, that hoarding money *finally enslaves*. He says that "No man can serve two masters; for either he will hate the one and love the other, or else he will hold to the one and despise the other. Ye cannot serve God and Mammon." He employs two significant words—the one, *Mammon* (an old Chaldaic word for the god of wealth); the other, *to serve*, the subjection of the slave to the caprice of an owner. Our Lord puts in juxtaposition the two masters—God the Beneficent Father, and Mammon the god of wealth, and says everyone must choose between them. Whichever you elect to serve will become the supreme dominating force in your life, giving you no option, save the obedience of a slave.

Notice then the peril of the Christian man who is falling under the sway of covetousness, which the Apostle calls idolatry (Col. iii. 5; Eph. v. 5). At the end of the process, be it longer or shorter, he will renounce entirely the service of God, and become the slave of money-making. The slightest acquaintance with commercial circles will give evidence of the tyranny of Mammon, which compels its abject slaves to toil day and night; demands the sacrifice of love and health, of home enjoyments and natural pleasures; insists that every interest shall be subordinate to its all-consuming service; and at the end of life casts its votary, bankrupt and penniless, upon the shores of eternity.

Drink itself, stripping men of everything worth living for, is not more to be dreaded.

.    .    .    .    .

WHAT, THEN, IS THE ALTERNATIVE to this prohibited hoarding of money? Are we to give away promiscuously and to everyone that asks? I confess that I have no faith in this indiscriminate giving which demoralises him who gives and him who receives; which creates a plentiful harvest of loafers and ne'er-do-wells, to the detriment of the thrifty and industrious poor, and which satisfies the sentiment of pity by a lazy dole, when it ought to set itself to a radical amelioration of the suppliant beggar. It is comparatively fruitless to give a meal here and there, without endeavouring, by practical sympathy and helping hand, to assist families by putting them in the way of helping themselves. This is what is needed; and to put individuals or housefuls in the way of standing upon their own feet and securing their own livelihood, is immensely more important than to furnish temporary relief, that supplies the need of to-day, but makes no permanent alteration in the circumstances of to-morrow or of the future. It is much more difficult to use our money thoughtfully and thriftily to help others than to place half-a-crown or a sovereign in their hands.

Here, for instance, is a poor woman, whose case appeals to to your sympathy. It is, of course, quite easy to give her a few shillings and to dismiss her from your mind, but the noblest thing would be to secure her a sewing-machine or a mangle, thus furnishing her with the opportunity of self-help. It is quite as important not to give money indiscriminately as it is not to hoard. The ideal method of life is to *use* what you have to help others, to regard your possession of money as a stewardship for the welfare of the the world, and to consider yourself a trustee for all who need. Instead of letting your dresses hang in the wardrobe,

give them to the respectable poor whose own are
threadbare, that they may be able to occupy suitably the
positions on which their livelihood depends. This is the
best way of keeping them free from moth. Whatever you
have in the way of books, recreation, spare rooms, elegantly
furnished homes, look upon them all as so many opportuni-
ties of helping and blessing others.

If you are in business, at the end of the year put aside
what is needed for the maintenance of your family in the
position to which God has called them; next, put aside
what may be required for the development of your business; third, be sure that by a system of life insurance you
you are providing for the failure of old age; but when all
this is done, look upon the remainder as God's, to be used
for Him. Never give God less than a tenth, but give Him
as much more as possible. If you have money by inheritance, you have no right to give that away or squander it;
but pass it down as you received it, always considering, if
you will, that the interest is God's, awaiting your adminis-
tration as His steward and trustee.

Let every Christian adopt the principle of giving a certain proportion of the income to the cause of Christ, and
whenever the fascination of money begins to assert itself,
instantly make a handsome donation to some needy cause.
Every time the temptation comes to look at money from a
selfish standpoint, meet it by looking up to God and saying:
" I thank Thee that Thou hast given me these things richly
to enjoy, and desire wisdom and grace to use them for
Thee and Thine."

WHAT WILL BE THE RESULT of a spiritual attitude like
this ? Ah, the full blessedness cannot be put in words—but
this you will find, you will have treasure in heaven ; for what
you invest in ministering to others is capital laid up in God's

Bank, the interest of which will always be accruing to you. I have a very distinct belief that actual interest comes from money which is being invested in doing good; and at last those we have helped will welcome us into the eternal mansions (Luke xvi. 9). Moreover, your heart will be increasingly fixed where your treasure is, in the Unseen and the Eternal. Your eye will be single, your life harmonious, your hold upon earthly things slender, your love for your Master, Christ, becoming a passion. Ultimately you will find that the yearning which you used to have for selfish satisfaction and comfort will pass away, as the blessing of him that was ready to perish falls upon your head, and the thanks of the widow and orphan anticipate the "Well done!" of your Lord.

# XVI

# The Intention of the Soul.

## (MATT. vi. 22.)

THE eye is the most striking and important feature in the face. Blue as the azure of heaven, brown as hazel, black as jet, it gives expression and beauty to the countenance, fills with tears of pity, sparkles with the radiance of affection, and flashes with the fire of anger. By the eye we are able, therefore, to discern much of the thoughts and intents of the heart.

The eye is also urgently needed to enable us to do the work of life. It is by the eye that we are lighted to our toils, discover the path in which we must tread, and look upon the faces of our friends, or the beauty of God's creation. Each time we see a blind person, or pass institutions devoted for the recovery of sight, let us lift up our hearts to thank God for this priceless boon.

It is interesting to notice the comparison which our Lord employs. He speaks of the eye as the "light of the body"; in other places, the same Greek word is rendered "lamp," or "candle." In the fifth chapter of Matthew we discover the same expression: "Neither do men light a lamp and put it under the bushel." The same word is used in Luke xii.: "Let your loins be girded about, and your lamps burning." It is the word by which John the Baptist is designated in John v.: "He was a burning and a shining light"—in contradistinction to the other term, applied to our Lord alone: "That was the true Light which

lighteth every man that cometh into the world." The
ministry of John was the lamp that lighted the steps of
men until " the Sun of Righteousness arose with healing in
His wings." The eye, our Lord says, is the lamp of the
house of the body. It is as though He thought of the eye
as hanging in the vestibule of the palace of life, casting its
rays outwards to the busy thoroughfare, and inward to the
recesses of the soul.

.        .        .        .        .        .

It is obvious that there must be something in our inner
life which corresponds to the eye, for our Lord adverts to
the eye as the emblem and symbol of something within.
He is not speaking of the eye of the body only, but of its
correlative, the eye of the soul.

What is that inner eye ? Some have supposed that it is
the power of a concentrated affection, for truly love sheds a
warm glow over all the furniture of the inner life, as well
as upon the great world without. Others have affirmed
that the intellect is the eye of the soul, by which we are
able to behold the ordered process of the world, and to consider the processes of thought within us. A truer conception of our Lord's meaning, however, will lead to the
conclusion that the eye of the body corresponds to the
inward intention and purpose of the soul.

If, for a moment, you will examine your inner life,
descending to the profound depths that lie beneath the surface of your being, you will discover that there is one deep
aim or purpose which is the real intention of your life.
Deep down, below the play of emotion and intellect, and of
engagement in various interests, there is one strong stream
or current running perpetually through the dark ravines of
your nature. It may be that you are hardly aware of it ;
your nearest and dearest friends do not realize it. You
would be startled if it were stated in so many words, but it

is none the less true, that there is a unity in each human character which God perceives. In each of us He can read a unity of purpose and a unity of will. This is the intention of the soul, and distinguishes each of us from everyone beside.

The eye may of course be healthy or unhealthy. If healthy, a tiny curtain which hangs at the back of the organism is adjusted to receive the focussed rays which come from external objects. On this tiny curtain is formed an inverted image of all things which are visible. If you look into the eye of another, and especially into the eye of a little babe, you will see the whole panorama of the world presented as in a *cinematoscope*. This curtain is perpetually being readjusted, so that the unblurred image of the outer world may be cast upon it. When we are travelling in a railway train it is probable that in a single hour the focus is altered thousands of times, for at every jolt and oscillation of the vehicle there must be a readjustment of the lens.

When the eye is in an unhealthy condition, the image is doubled or blurred. There are two ways in which it may become evil. To use a common expression, there may be the obliquity called a squint, such as disfigured the noble face of Edward Irving. Mrs. Oliphant tells us that as a babe he was laid in a wooden cradle, through a hole in which he was able to watch the light with one eye, whilst the other retained its usual straightforward direction. His eyes, therefore, were not parallel, and it was impossible to focus them upon a given object. The soul's intention may be diverted from a single purpose in a double direction. We may pray with the object of gaining an answer from God, and at the same time of receiving credit from man. We may try to amass the treasures of this world, and at the same time to be rich towards God. We may endeavour to serve two masters—God and Mammon. This is the counterpart in the spiritual life of a squint in the eye.

Another source of ill-health with the eye is when the little vesicles, which supply blood for the tiny curtain, become overcharged, so that it is impossible for the delicate nerves to adjust the lens, and the vision becomes blurred and indistinct.

Yet another source of the evil eye is when a film forms over the surface of the pupil, so that the light cannot enter.

In contradistinction to all these evils, how good it is to have a clear eye, with its distinct vision ; and how much more good it is, when the purpose and intention of the soul is so undivided that the whole of life is illumined by the glow of a clear and beautiful radiance. All through this chapter our Lord is arguing against this double vision. He says : " Do not profess to belong to the kingdom of heaven while your hearts are buried in the earth ; do not have two masters ; do not be divided by anxious care ; seek first the kingdom of God." All through this chapter He is, in fact, bidding us to make our constant prayer the cry of the Psalmist : " Unite my heart to fear Thy Name." Our Lord sets His whole force against any duplication of character so inimitably described by John Bunyan, in Mr. Facing-both-ways, who, with one eye on heaven and another on earth, sincerely professed one thing and sincerely did another, and from the inveteracy of his unreality was unable to see the contradiction of his life. " He tried to cheat both God and the Devil, and in reality he only cheated himself and his neighbours."

There are THREE KINDS OF MEN. First, those who have no intention. Second, those who have a double intention. Third, those whose intention is pure and simple.

(1) *Some have no intention.* They live day by day without purpose; the eye of the mind is fixed definitely and intently upon nothing. They take each day as it comes, getting from it anything it may bring, doing the duty it demands; but their existence is from hand to mouth, at haphazard, with no aim, no ambition, no godly purpose. They cannot say, with the Apostle, that they are leaving the things which are behind, and pressing forward to the things which are before, or that one thing they are ever engaged in doing. It is quite true that in many cases there may be no great cause to be championed, no subjects to be explored, no object in making money, because already there is an ample competence. Some may read these words who are daughters in a wealthy home, or young men, the heirs of a considerable fortune, or people in humble life who have no urgent need to look beyond the day or week with its ordinary routine; but even these should have a supreme purpose, to bring down the New Jerusalem out of heaven, to establish the kingdom of God amongst men, to hasten the coming of the day of Christ, or to be themselves purer and holier. To *become* may always be the supreme purpose and intention of the soul; to be a little more like Christ; to know and love Him better; to be able to shed more of His sweetness and strength upon others. There is no life so contained within the high walls of circumstances, but it may reach up towards the profound light of the azure sky that arches above.

Do not be content to drift through life; do not be satisfied to be a piece of flotsam, swept to and fro by the ebb and flow of the stream; do not be a creature of circumstance; because it is certain that if you are not living with a Divine purpose for God and eternity, you are as certainly living for yourself, for your ease, for mere indolent enjoyment, or to get through the years with as little fret and friction as possible. This, at the heart of it, and in such a world as this, so abject and needy, is undiluted selfishness. To have no purpose is to have the worst purpose; to have no ambition is to be living for self; to have no intention is to be drifting through the wide gate, in company with the many that go in thereat, to their own destruction.

. . . . . .

(2) *Some have a double intention.* They have heard the call of Christ, and have received the seed of the kingdom; but, so soon as it reached their hearts, two strong competitors endeavoured to share with it the nutriment of the soul. On the one hand there were the cares of the world—these largely have place in the poor and struggling; on the other hand was the deceitfulness of riches—these principally are found among the opulent and well to do. For a brief interval there was a struggle as to which of these should be master, but the strife soon ended in the victory of the sturdy thorns: those ruthless brigands seized for themselves all the sustenance that the soil of the heart could supply, and grew ranker and taller, until the tiny corn withered and failed to bring forth fruit to perfection.

Will you not examine yourself? You think that you are whole-hearted, whereas you may be double-hearted; or, to use the apt simile of the prophet, baked on one side and not on the other; or, to use the simile of the great dreamer, looking one way and rowing another. You seem to be very earnest in Christian work, but are you quite sure that your apparent devotion does not arise from a masterfulness of disposition that likes to be independent and rule? May it not be due to a fussy activity, which must be engaged in many directions that the soul may escape from itself; or to a natural pity and sympathy for men, which would incite you to do a similar deed even though you had never heard of Christ? Of course, you say to yourself that your motive is pure and single, and that you only desire to glorify God; but in His sight it may be that you are really actuated by the natural propensities of your nature, by your desire to be first, or by your appetite for notoriety or money. The heart is so deceitful that it becomes us to examine ourselves with all carefulness, lest at the end of life we shall find that whilst we appeared to be doing God's work, we were really doing our own; and that whilst our friends gave us credit for great religious devotion, we were really borne along by a vain, proud, and unworthy purpose, which robbed our noblest service of all value in the sight of eternity.

As the Apostle says, the one supreme intention of every child of God should be to please God. How few of us can say with him: "Whose I am and whom I serve!" "It is a very small thing that I should be judged of you, or of man's judgment; He that judgeth me is the Lord."

. . . . . .

(3) Let us see to it that we have *a pure and simple intention*. Our aim should be to set our whole soul upon one thing only—to do the will of God, so that the whole of our religious life may be spent before the Father, who seeth in secret; that our alms, our prayers, our fastings, should be for His eye, and His alone; and that the whole of our life should emanate from hidden fountains where God's Spirit broods, like those fountains of the Nile concealed in the heart of the great mountains, the secret of which has so long defied the research of the explorer. The lamp of a holy life is the pure intention of the soul, which seeks to gain nothing for itself; which has no desire to please men, or to receive their commendation; which does not shirk adversity or court the sunshine, but which sets before it, as

its all-sufficient goal, that God may be well-pleased, and that at the close of life's brief pilgrimage it may be said of each of us, as it was said of Enoch: "He had this testimony, that he pleased God."

How blessed such a life is! The light of the soul's pure intention illuminates God, duty, human love, the glory of creation, and the significance of history, literature, and art. I remember once in my life, at a most important crisis, when for weeks I was so torn between two strong conflicting claims, that at last I was compelled to put aside all engagements and to go alone into the midst of Nature, where I carefully examined my heart to its very depths. I found that the cause of the difficulty to ascertain God's will arose because I allowed so many personal considerations to conflict with the inner voice; and when I definitely put these aside, and stilled and quieted my life so that I became conscious of being impelled by one purpose only—to know and to do God's will—then the lamp of a pure intention shed its glow upon the path which I became assured was the chosen path for me. And since I dared from that moment to follow, all other things have been added. It was when Solomon asked that he might have a wise and understanding heart, that he might know God's purpose, that God gave him honour, wealth, and length of days. Again and again these words of Christ ring out as amongst the deepest that He ever spoke: "Seek ye first the Kingdom of God and His righteousness, and all these things shall be added unto you."

.    .    .    .    .    .

If the lamp of the pure intention of the soul is not kept pure and clean, "how great is the darkness!" Our Lord alludes, of course, to the fact that when darkness settles upon the forest, the beasts steal forth, the glades resound to the roar of the lion, the cry of the jackal, the laugh of the hyena. Multitudes of beasts have lain quiet in

their lairs whilst the sun was shining creep forth : and our
Lord says that when a man's heart is set on doing God's
will the lower and baser passions of his nature—like so
many beasts of prey—remain in their hiding-places; but as
soon as the blur comes, and the soul ceases to live for
the one intense purpose of pleasing God, then darkness
steals upon the house of life, and all manner of evil and
unclean things, that otherwise would be shamed into silence
and secrecy, begin to reveal themselves. "How great is
that darkness!" If I am addressing men who are conscious
that there is a darkness upon life, upon truth, upon the
Word of God; if they are perplexed and plagued by the
intrusion of evil things which fill them with misgiving—let
me urge them to ask God to "cleanse the thoughts of their
hearts by the inspiration of His Holy Spirit, that they
may perfectly love Him, and worthily magnify His Holy
Name."

# XVII

# The Lesson of Birds and Flowers.

(MATT. vi. 25–34.)

THE eye—that is, the pure intention—of the soul ceases to be single when it is diverted by the covetous desire to hoard up money. It may also be diverted by the constant pressure of anxiety. As, therefore, our Lord has been dealing with avarice, which is the special temptation of the well to do and prosperous, so now He turns to deal with the special temptation of the poor, which is anxious care.

Of course, wealth has its anxieties as well as poverty. The rich man, whose wealth may be swept away in an hour by a panic on the Stock Exchange, may toss on a sleepless pillow, whilst the labouring man, who cannot see beyond the needs of the week, may be sleeping soundly through the small hours. But the anxiety of those who, in any event, will always be certain of being provided with the necessaries of life is surely less excusable than the care of the poor man, who has no nest-egg against a rainy day; who may at any moment fall sick or lose his situation, and who may be condemned to see first his home, and then his scanty wardrobe, stripped first of little comforts, and then of necessaries; and, when all is gone, his wife and children becoming every day paler, thinner, and hungrier.

. . . . . .

It is to be noticed that our Lord's tone is much gentler and more tender as He turns to address the poor, who toil for their daily bread, and whose slenderly provided table is often shadowed with the spectre of anxiety about to-morrow's provision. In the former paragraph there was a

tone of stern remonstrance as He spoke of the absurdity of
setting the heart on things which the thief might steal and
the moth corrupt; but here there is a touch of tender pity
and sympathy, as He says, three times over: "Don't be
anxious." He never forgot that He was the child of the
labouring classes; that His mother, at His birth, had
brought the gift of the poor to the Temple; and that, from
boyhood, He had been accustomed to the shifts of poverty.
His frequent speech about patching garments and using old
bottleskins, about the price of sparrows, and the scanty
pittance of a labourer's life, indicate that His mind was
habituated to the experiences of the poor. Ever since He
had left His mother's home, abandoning the trade which
had secured slender provision for Himself and others, He
had known what it was to have no place in which to shelter
for the night, and to subsist on the chance gifts of charity
and friendship.

The words "take no thought," in the Authorized Version,
do not represent the true force of the phrase as used by our
Lord. We are endowed with the faculty of foresight, of
scanning the horizon, of anticipating the lowering storm-
clouds, and of taking in our sails. "He that provideth
not for his own," says the Apostle, "is worse than an
unbeliever"—and provision involves foresight. But there
is all the difference in the world between foresight and
foreboding. It is the latter, not the former, that our Lord
chides. A wise man must lay his carefully considered
plans, and work for their accomplishment. The farmer
must sow in the autumn for the coming harvest. The
importer must arrange, months beforehand, for the arrival
of foreign produce at a given time when the home markets
will be ripe for it. The manufacturer is already preparing
the season's goods for next year. But when all has been

done that can be done, our Lord says: "You must leave the results with God: you have done all that you could do; now leave the outcome with your heavenly Father."

The words which are suggested by the Revised Version, instead of "Take no thought," are "Be not anxious." The Greek word implies that the mind is divided and broken up from the main object and purpose of existence, by the constant pressure of foreboding care. As the force of a stream is lessened if the waters are diverted into two or three channels, so the force of heart and life dwindle when the perpetual dread of failure and loss calls off the soul from its primary intention and aim. How can a man do his best work if he is paralysed by foreboding as to the contents of to-morrow! When the mind is stricken with panic, tossed to and fro with distraction, and filled with pictures of penury and destitution; when every sight of wife and family only awakens deeper dread of what may await them; when paragraphs in the daily papers prophesy the pressure of hard times—how can the soul do its best work? It is divided, distracted, and torn.

.     .     .     .     .     .

In this paragraph our Lord is dealing principally with food and raiment—the simple needs of an agricultural and pastoral people. And there are myriads around us on whose lips these questions are perpetual. "What shall we eat? What shall we drink? Wherewithal shall we be clothed?" Clearly we are creatures of two worlds. Our minds hunger for truth and our hearts for love. "Man doth not live by bread alone." And there are anxieties for others, for their clothing in the garments of purity and holiness, for their feeding on the fare of the truth of God, and for their housing in the love of God, which are far more pressing and imperative than the care for their physical and temporal well-being. All these dividing thoughts are equally forbidden when our Lord says: "Do not be anxious."

*     *     *     *     *     *

Three times over we hear this sweet refrain, *Be not anxious*, 25–30 ; *Be not therefore anxious*, 31–33 ; *Be not therefore anxious*, 34.

*     *     *     *     *     *

Do not be Anxious about Food, whether of the Body, the Mind, or the Heart. (1) " *The life is more than the food* " (25). When God gave life, He caused it to be dependent on the sustenance which is provided from field and orchard. It is by His own contrivance and ordering that we must be nourished by the fruits of the soil ; and surely He will not be so unreasonable as to create the need and to contrive the perpetual recurrence of appetite, and then to fail in meeting both. If He has given life, does not that gift implicate its support? He must have had a purpose in the donation of life to any one of us ; and surely He will be responsible for the food which is necessary, if His original purpose is not to be frustrated?

(2) *Are ye not of much more value than the birds of the heaven?* As our Lord was speaking, flocks of pigeons were flying overhead ; swallows were darting in the air for insects ; sparrows were flying, chirping, from stone to stone in search of food. All this wonderful and multitudinous bird-life, so blithe and happy, was a matter of constant interest to the child-heart of Jesus, and seemed to rebuke foreboding fear. These little feathered creatures do not perform a stroke of work for their living. They do not provide their food, but only take what the Creator gives, as He opens His hand to supply their need. That which He giveth them they gather. You may walk for days through the forests and find no dead bird. I grant you that the wild things of the woods do perish at certain

seasons; but, before we charge this on any want of care on the part of the Creator, it would have to be shown that the balance of creation had not been disturbed by human interference. Do we not prognosticate the advent of a hard winter by the abundance of berries on the hedges, and is not that the Divine provision for the birds of the air, who have neither storehouse nor barn? Surely, if our heavenly Father feeds these tiny creatures, which are the pensioners on His bounty, and can do nothing to help themselves, He will not be unmindful of His children! "Your heavenly Father feedeth them—are ye not much better than they?"

(3) Besides, "*Which of you by being anxious can add one cubit unto his stature?*" or (as the margin suggests) to his *age*. Clearly the Lord is not speaking of our physical stature, for it would be an unheard-of thing, and one for which none would be specially solicitous, to add a foot and a half to his stature! He is evidently alluding to the length of human life, of which the Psalmist says: "Thou hast made my days as an handbreadth." After all, the length of our years has been fixed by God; and we are immortal till our work is done. All our anxiety will not add an inch or a yard to the path that we are destined to tread between our cradle and our grave. God has measured it out with exact precision, and He will supply all our need until the day's march is ended, and the day's labour fulfilled.

.    .    .    .    .    .

DO NOT BE ANXIOUS ABOUT CLOTHING. (1) All the *animals have their covering*, the lamb its wool, the kitten its fur, the fledgling its fluffy down—but man is born naked, and requires clothing for modesty and warmth. This was evidently the intention of the Creator, and He has filled the world with the materials for our supply. May we not hold Him responsible to meet the needs of His own creation? Did He not clothe Adam and Eve with the skins of beasts already slain in sacrifice? Does He not provide for the soul the white and dazzling raiment of imputed righteousness, with which we are arrayed before all worlds? And will He neglect the body? "The body is more than raiment." If He bestows the one so curiously and wondrously wrought, surely He will give the other.

(2) Besides, look again into *nature at the growth of the flowers*. At the time when Jesus spoke, the fields were carpeted with wild flowers. Palestine in those days was the land, not of milk only, bespeaking the rich pastures, but of honey, because the air was redolent with the breath of myriads of wild flowers, bespangling the pastures, clustering in the hedgerows, and hiding in the woodland glades. Theirs was as careless a life as that of the birds. "They toil not, neither do they spin." For some, no doubt— the exotics of our greenhouses and nurseries—there must be excessive care, in the provision of greenhouse heat and the experienced skill of the horticulturist. The Lord was not alluding to these, but to the flowers of the grass, which grew amid the wilds of nature or in the gardens of the poor, and were cut down by the scythe or gathered to perish quickly in the hot hand of the careless child. To Him these were exquisitely beautiful. Of the Son of Man it may be said, with peculiar appropriateness, that "the meanest flower that blew awakened thoughts too deep for tears." The wild flowers of His native land were, in His eyes, attired in garments more rare and beautiful than the gorgeous magnificence of Israel's greatest king. "Solomon in all his glory was not arrayed like one of these." How quietly they grew, far apart from the clatter of machinery, the throw of the shuttle, the revolution of the wheel! How modestly and unobtrusively they concealed themselves from the glare of publicity, in dells and woodland glades! How simple in their chaste and lovely garb!

What do they teach?   Was not this the lesson of their growth, that God loves the beautiful, and expends thought and skill in its production?   He might have made the world without a daisy, and human life without childhood. Considerations of stern utility might have imposed their rigorous law on the creation of all things visible and invisible; but since the Creator clothes with beauty the short-lived flowers of the wilds, the ephemeral insects of a summer day, the shells of the minute creatures that build up the solid fabric of the rocks, by the countless myriads of their tiny homes, surely this prodigality, this lavishness, this prolific superabundance of creativeness, must mean that He can and will withhold no good thing from them that fear Him, least of all clothes for their nakedness and warmth.

Of course we must fulfil our part.   We are not to imitate the careless improvident life of the lower orders of creation. We must certainly sow and reap and gather into barns; we must certainly toil if we are men, and spin if we are women; but when we have done all, we must fall back on the Divine Providence, believing that it is vain for us to rise up early, and sit up late, and eat the bread of sorrows, because our God will give us all we need, even whilst we sleep.   He will not allow His children to starve, or go unsheltered, unclothed, and unshod.   "Therefore, take no thought, saying, What shall we eat, or what shall we drink, or wherewithal shall we be clothed?"

BE NOT ANXIOUS: *it is Heathenish.*   "After all these things do the Gentiles seek."   The blue waters of the Mediterranean were almost within sight, reminding the Speaker of the great nations that lay around their shores, and launched their navies on their bosom.   He knew that whilst some might be feeling after God, if haply they might find Him, or be found of Him, the bulk of them had refused to retain Him in their knowledge, and had exchanged the Creator for the creature. He knew, moreover, that to most of them either there was no God or they deemed Him too far removed from sublunary things to have any interest in their lives. Of what good, then, was it to pray to Him? For many the supreme conception was of fate, destiny, or chance, as the presiding arbiter and ruler of their existence.

Amid the darkness of such conceptions, what could be expected but that the grim spectre of care should haunt every life, and sit uninvited at every table. When man has no knowledge of the Divine Fatherhood, what defence has he against sudden, wild alarms, or insidious corroding care?

But those whom our Lord addressed had been taught to regard God as their Heavenly Father; and to us the revelation has been more explicit than ever to them. We know that we are sons of God, begotten unto a living hope, partakers of the Divine nature, adopted into the Divine family. We are conscious that the spirit of sonship is in our hearts, witnessing that we have been born from above. We realize that we are not only sons but heirs—heirs of God and joint heirs with Christ. Our Father loves us, knows our frame, views us with paternal pitifulness, and longs to bring us to glory. He has given us His Son and His Spirit: surely He will not withhold the food and raiment of our body. He has given the infinitely great; surely He will not grudge the small. "He that spared not His own Son, but delivered Him up for us all, how shall He not with Him also freely give us all things?"

.  .  .  .  .  .

BE NOT ANXIOUS: *there are other and greater Interests at Stake.* "Seek ye first the kingdom of God and His righteousness." It is the great object of God that His

long-expected Kingdom should come; that purity as of
the dawn should replace the reign of corruption and
night; that joyous life should replace death, and love
hatred. For this He has been at work all through the
long centuries, nor will He stay His hand till angel-voices
proclaim that the kingdoms of this world have become the
kingdoms of His Christ.

In His great kindness He has called us in to help Him
accomplish His high purpose, and lays it upon us as a
special burden that we should not rest, nor allow Him to
rest, until the Kingdom come, and His will be done on
earth as in heaven. For this we must labour and pray.
Be anxious for this, if you will. Lie awake at night to
mourn over the condition of lost souls, if you can. Expend
tears and prayers in untiring supplication for the lost.
Whilst you care for God's concerns, God will care for yours.

The great contractor who has undertaken a line of railway, or the construction of a vast reservoir among the
hills, knows the necessity of providing for the well-being
of the thousands of navvies engaged with their spades or
trowels. If they are to do work which will not dis-
grace him, he at least must see that their physical health
and well-being are guaranteed. Is it likely, then, that God
will be less careful and thoughtful of His own sons, whom
He has called into fellowship with Himself? Does He not
know that we shall do our best work when we are free
from anxious care? Is He so unrighteous as to forget us,
who labour day and night for the purpose which lies so
near His heart? It is impossible to suppose it; but as we
seek His Kingdom, He will seek our welfare, with both
hands, earnestly and carefully. Rest on this promise,
which He gave who is incarnate truth: "All these things
shall be added."

Be not Anxious: *it will not Rob to-morrow of its Anxiety, though it will deprive to-day of its Strength.* "Take, therefore, no thought for the morrow, for the morrow will be anxious for itself. Sufficient unto the day is the evil thereof." From these words it is clear that every morrow will have some anxiety, and every day some evil. No sky without some clouds to fleck its blue, no lot without its crook, no Paschal lamb without its bitter herbs. We shall never be totally free from anxiety of one kind or another until we have passed the gates of pearl.

However much we worry to-day, in the hope of anticipating and cancelling the worry of to-morrow, we shall not succeed. There always will be something to cause us annoyance, perplexity, and chagrin. But as the day, so will the strength be—just enough, with not one grain to spare. Indeed, the anxiety will be permitted to drive us to the strong for strength, as a hard winter will drive even the timid deer down to the homes of men.

To worry, therefore, about to-morrow is to overpress the strength of to-day, which is enough for to-day's burden, but not enough for to-day's and to-morrow's also. If you try to carry to-day's burdens by actual endurance, and to-morrow's by anticipation, what wonder that you break down, ageing prematurely, and sowing plentiful silver among the black locks of young manhood.

. . . . . .

For all these reasons, let us not be anxious. "Be careful for nothing, but in everything by prayer and supplication, with thanksgiving, let your requests be made known unto God; and the peace of God, which passeth all understanding, shall keep your hearts and minds, through Christ Jesus."

# XVIII

# "To Them that are Without."

(MATT. vii. 1-6.)

AS long as we are in this mortal life, we shall necessarily come into contact with those whose lives are
godless and evil. Evil men and seducers will wax
worse and worse. People will always abound who will not
consent to wholesome words, even the words of our Lord
Jesus Christ, and the doctrine which is according to godliness. There will always be perverse disputings of men
of corrupt minds, destitute of the truth, and enemies to
whatever is pure, lovely, holy, and of good report. In this
paragraph of the Sermon on the Mount, our Lord sets
Himself to show us how to act towards such. It is clear
that the Master had no desire that His servants should
retire from human society, but should live amongst men as
salt and light, arresting the progress of corruption, and
abashing the evil deeds that hide under the cover of
darkness; but, in addition to the quiet influence of our
character, there will always be scope for a further exercise
of Christian principle. In what direction, and to what
extent, is this to take effect, and by what laws is it to be
governed? In answer to these questions our Lord lays
down a general principle, which is removed as far as
possible from that which obtains among men. He says:
"Whatever you do, think, or say about others must be in
precise accordance with what you would like them to do,
think, or say about yourself. Judge not, for with what
judgment ye judge, ye shall be judged. With what
measure ye mete, it shall be measured to you again. All

things whatsoever ye would that men should do unto you, do ye even so to them; and all things whatsoever ye would *not* that men should do unto you, do ye not so to them."

It is clear that there are in this paragraph three circles of men with whom we are constantly thrown into contact. First, our *Associates and Neighbours,* whose characters and conduct are constantly passing in review before us; secondly, *the Erring Ones,* whose motes trouble us; and, thirdly, *the Dogs and Swine,* which stand for the notoriously vicious and profane.

As to our Associates and Neighbours, (1) *Our Lord says:* "*Judge not.*" We need hardly say that there is a sense in which we are bound to form careful judgments on those around us. The judgment is one of the noblest faculties of our moral life, and our surest safeguard from the sharks that infest the seas. The young girl must use it, of the man who is seeking to engage her affections; the young man must use it, of the man who offers him a partnership; the seeker after truth must use it, of the teacher who professes to be able to lead him. There is no prayer that we need more often or more fervently to make than that God would give us right judgment in all things. "He that is spiritual judgeth all things."

But the judgment prohibited by our Lord is altogether different from this, and is that spirit of censoriousness and unkindness which is always lying in wait for others, and making strong and uncharitable statements on the most superficial view of their words and actions, without trying to understand the motives by which they have been actuated or the difficulties of their position.

The natural man is proud, haughty, and self-opinionated. He has a great contempt of, and a great prejudice towards, those who do not belong to his own sect or party. He is, therefore, constantly on the watch for them, making faults where there are none, and aggravating them where they are. When he has formed, however hastily, his judgment, he is not content with contemplating it for himself, but takes every opportunity of venting it in word and act. If such men can win another to their party, they are perfectly willing to condone his faults; otherwise they will not scruple to antagonise him and his influence, by poisoning the minds of his neighbours and contemporaries. This sin of censorious judgment is a constant peril to us all, and one against which we need to watch and pray.

Beware lest you have a secret joy in seeing that another, who had borne an irreproachable character, has failed! Beware lest you base your estimate of another on idle stories, suspicions, suggestions, and surmises, and without sufficient evidence! Beware of seeking after a reputation for quickness in estimating the true worth of others, since the desire to maintain such a reputation is fraught with temptation! Beware of speaking of the faults of others, except you have prayed about them first! Beware of uttering your criticisms, unless there is some end to be gained in warning others! Beware of speaking of others; till you have looked at home! Remember the proverb about glass houses!

There are some who seem unable of forming a generous estimate of any. According to them, there is always some evil motive behind apparent goodness, which detracts from all merit or virtue. "Yes, he does seem religious and humane, but then, you know, there is a rich old relative in the background, and it is all-important to keep in touch with him, and that sort of thing goes down well in that quarter." Or, "Yes, he is religious enough just now, but, you know, there is a lady in the question, and he is perfectly right in the way he is taking to win her." Ah, it is a sad and miserable state of mind to have no eyes but for wounds, and bruises, and putrefying sores, and to find these beneath the surface when they do not appear to the eyes of others. There are many young men and women amongst us in society who can hardly indulge in any language but that of depreciation.

(2) *Our ignorance of most of the facts* should give us pause before passing harsh and censorious judgments. Take this, for instance : A merchant was thought to be very selfish with his money. He was known to be very rich, and yet when asked for subscriptions he gave always a small sum (£5) where his neighbours thought he ought to give £20. He was therefore in ill odour for miserliness and greed. This went on for years, and many closed their hearts against him. One of his friends, however, who felt that there might be some other explanation, set himself, with careful inquiry, to ascertain the facts. It was with some difficulty that he finally discovered that this much-abused man was supporting handsomely a large family of poor relatives. He educated them well, and put them out in life with no niggard hand. They lived in another town, and no one knew of the source of their income. Their benefactor never allowed his left hand to know what his right hand did. Here was a man whom all were mis-judging because they did not know the full facts. Is it a solitary instance ?

(3) *The fact that we cannot judge others adversely without revealing ourselves* may also make us hesitate. The man who imputes low motives to the conduct of another, is probably conscious of their presence within himself. He is already actuated by them, or would be if he were in the place of the man he criticises. He has no higher standard for another than that which rules in his own breast, and almost unconsciously in his criticisms he is revealing his secret soul.

(4) *It is inevitable that our harsh judgments of others
will come back on ourselves.* A man receives back what he
gives. There is an automatic law of compensation in
society. Kindness begets kindness, censoriousness begets
censoriousness. Ishmael's hand was against everyone, and
every man's hand was against him. Adonibezek cut off
the thumbs and great toes of seventy kings; and as it was
done by him it was done to him. Haman was hanged on
the gallows which he had erected for Mordecai. The Jew,
who banned all men as heathen dogs, is himself banned.
The world may fitly be compared to a vast field in which
each man drops his seed, and it comes back to him, not just
the same that it was when he dropped it in, any more than
in the autumn you reap from the earth the black berry
which you hid in its broad bosom in the spring, but something which has its true correspondence and proportion to
that. Every gift has its return, every act its rebound, every
voice its echo. The Lord states the alternative in another
discourse, closely corresponding to this, when He says :
" Give, and it shall be given unto you ; good measure,
pressed down, and shaken together, and running over, shall
men give into your bosom. For with the same measure
that ye mete withal it shall be measured to you again."

" Wherefore judge nothing before the time, until the
Lord come, who will both bring to light the hidden things
of darkness, and make manifest the counsels of the hearts,
and then shall each man have his praise from God "
(1 Cor. iv. 5, R.V.). Especially guard against *prejudice*—
that is, pre-judgment. Remember that there are dogs and
swine in the make-up of your own heart, and you must
see to it that their presence does not trample under feet
what is purest, noblest, and best, and rend men and women
who, if you but knew and understood them more fully,
would attract your loving veneration. Remember the

words with which our Lord prefaced His warning against
censorious judgment: " Be ye therefore merciful, as your
Father also is merciful."

. . . . . .

As to the Erring—(1) *Consider the beam that is in your
own eye.* The beam is, of course, a log, rafter, or joist, and
is the extreme contrast to the chip or splint of wood which
is light enough to float in the air ; and a child can understand what our Lord means when He employs a well-
known Jewish proverb to give the flavour of homeliness to
His speech.

(2) *By nature we are extremely prone to put other people
right.* We behold the mote that is in our brother's eye
till we can think of nothing else. All the good qualities
he possesses weigh lighter than swansdown against that
one inconsistency which presents itself to us at each mention
of his name. Finally, we go to him with the fixed resolve
of ridding him of his mote, saying : " Let me pull out the
mote that is in thine eye." Now in all this there would be
nothing to condemn—indeed, there would be much to
commend—if it were done lovingly, humbly, and after the
due confession and putting away from our own life of all
inconsistency and sin ; but it is the height of absurdity to
attempt to extract the mote when your own vision is dis-
torted by the presence of the unextracted beam. How dare
you presume to deal with the faultiness of others, when your
own faults have not been corrected ! It is like Satan re-
buking sin. Well may men cry, " Physician, heal thyself."

(3) *It is evidently a very delicate operation to correct the
faults of others.* Our Lord compares it to the extraction of
a little piece of grit, or dust, or a minute insect, from an
inflamed eye. A clumsy hand may easily make the matter
worse. Only the tenderest, strongest hand can be trusted
for the operation ; and, if I might choose, let me have one

who has himself suffered, being tempted. It is only He, who has been tempted in all points like as we are, though without sin, who can be trusted to deal with our inner temptations, inconsistencies, and failures. It is the man whose own transgressions have been forgiven according to the multitude of God's tender mercies who can teach transgressors His ways.

(4) *First cast out the beam out of thine own eye.* There is a beam there, if you only knew it. We look, it has been said, at our neighbour's errors with a microscope, but at our own through the wrong end of a telescope. We have two sets of weights and measures—one for home use, and the other for foreign. Every vice has two names; and we call it by the flattering and minimising one when *we* commit it, and by the ugly one when our neighbour does. Everybody can see the hump on his friend's shoulders, but it takes some effort to see our own. A blind guide is bad enough, but a blind oculist is a still more ridiculous anomaly. The more we know of ourselves, the more pitiful we shall be of others; the less likely to form rash and harsh judgments; the more sweet and tender we shall be in trying to make men better.

(5) *Then thou shalt see clearly.* Only the pure heart sees; and when once some heart-sin is put away a flood of light pours on all things in heaven and on earth. We see sin as we never saw it, and the love of God and the grace of our Lord Jesus Christ.

> Heaven above is softer blue,
>   Earth around is sweeter green ;
> Something shines in every hue
>   Christless eyes have never seen.
> Birds with gladder songs o'erflow,
>   Flowers with brighter beauties shine,
> While Christ whispers in my ear,
>   I am His and He is mine.

As to Dogs and Swine—*Use a wise discrimination*. Suppose a priest, on coming out of the Temple, encounters a hungry dog—one of those yelping, voracious, unclean animals, which are the scavengers and pests of Oriental cities—would it be seemly for him to return to the Temple, take a piece of the flesh which was reserved from the sacrifices for the use of priests, and therefore *holy*, and give it to the dog for food? He might relieve the creature's hunger, but not with such food as that. Or suppose a man, carrying a bag of pearls through a forest, were to encounter a hog, would it be wise or seemly for him to place the pearls before it, when it needed acorns? Similarly, it is unseemly to offer the sacraments of our holy religion, or the forgiveness of Christ's Gospel, to the notoriously unclean and untrue, or to discuss the sacred mysteries of the Epistle to the Ephesians with those who are set on coarse and carnal pleasures. Their natures must first be changed. They must be born from above. Old things must pass away, and all things become new. Then, when the heart of stone has been removed and the heart of flesh substituted, the soul will hunger after the Divine mysteries, and will be able to appreciate them in such a way as to justify us in presenting them. The raven may feed on carrion, but the dove will return to Noah's Ark until she can find her natural food.

.    .    .    .    .    .

For all this we need something which was not fully revealed when our Lord was speaking, but has been revealed since. The soul which stands before this high ideal is filled with despair until it remembers—first, that the precious Blood cleanses from all sin and shortcoming; and, second, that the Holy Spirit longs to make possible and real these heavenly ideals. May that Blood cleanse, and that Spirit renew and perfect thee and me!

# XIX

# The Royalty of our Life.

(MATT. vii. 7-12.)

IT is inevitable, as the Lord has clearly implied in the preceding words, that, so long as we are in the world, we must come in contact with its evil. There will be inconsistencies that we shall be tempted to judge, motes and beams that we shall have to extract, and swine or dogs with which we must reckon. It cannot be child's play for any of us. And if we are to keep ourselves unspotted from the world, and unsubdued by the inward power of sin, we must have resort to the weapon of All-Prayer. Therefore it is that our Lord turns from the exhortations of the preceding paragraph to these injunctions concerning prayer. It was as though He said : " You will never succeed in being or doing what I say, unless your lives are full of persistent and prevailing prayer."

It may be that there is an even wider range of thought. As we review this matchless conception of a holy life, so far removed above anything which the mind of man has conceived ; as we recall the Beatitudes of the opening sentences, the searching fulfilment of the older law, the warnings against an impaired intention of the soul, against ostentation, covetousness, and care—our hearts may well faint within us at the immensity of the task before us. And as we think of His demand—that we should be perfect as our heavenly Father is perfect, that we should be filled with a Divine love, and that we should always treat others as we wish that they should treat us—we might again cry : " Who is sufficient for these things ? " To answer this double

attitude, which is indeed one, the Lord says : " *Pray !*
What is impossible with man is possible with God.
Pray !"

We have here two words which prove that the entire
paragraph is closely jointed together : " If ye *then* being
evil "; " All things, *therefore,* whatsoever." The exhortation to prayer is followed by an analogy, and this by an
injunction.

. . . . . .

THE EXHORTATION TO PRAYER. (1) *Ask.* Our Master
knew well how much it would mean to us that His own lips
should utter that word, but He did not hesitate to speak it.
As Son of God, He knew all that asking would do for us ;
and, as Son of Man, He had often proved the value of the
practice He enjoined. *Ask,* He said. It was as though
He loved to dwell on the word. See ! He repeats it, not
once or twice, but four times over. " Everyone that
*asketh* receiveth "; " if his son shall *ask* for a loaf "; " if he
shall *ask* for a fish "; " good things to them that *ask.*" It
seems as though our Lord would do away with the formality
and stateliness that attach to too many of our prayers, and
teach us that praying is just asking, and asking as a child
would ask. Men shrink from asking for a favour from
their fellows, but a little child has no reserve with its
father. In the simplest and most artless manner it asks
for what it wants, and with no doubt at all that the father
will gladly hasten to respond. " Thus," says our Lord,
" ask God for what you want, as long ago you asked your
parents ; and do it without vehemence or self-conscious-
ness."

" Every one that asketh receiveth." Emerson tells us
that he preached his first sermon from these words, having
obtained his divisions from the blunt saying of a field
labourer, who said that men are always praying, and always

being heard. His divisions, therefore, were as follows :—
(1) Men are always praying; (2) all their prayers are
granted ; (3) we must beware, then, what we ask. The
second is the doubtful one. Is it true that all our prayers
are granted ? Not surely in the way that we ask, as we
shall see ; but in some way. There is no prayer that we
utter which is based on a real need—nothing that we
sincerely ask for which is not answered somehow, somewhen,
somewhere.

With too many of us, alas ! there is a failure in the art
of receptiveness. We ask, but we fail to take. We send
out our letter in the outgoing mail, but never go near the
office to ask if there is a reply addressed to us. We send
an ocean cablegram asking for a consignment of heavenly
treasure, but never go down to the wharf to ascertain if it
has arrived, and to claim it.

(2) *Seek.* You ask for a gift; you seek for something you
have lost, or for some valuable treasure. The miner gropes
along the corridors of the mine on his quest; the pearl-
fisher dives in search of goodly pearls; the woman who had
lost her silver piece lit a candle, and swept and searched
her house diligently till she found it. Seek, says our Lord.
If you have lost your peace with God, the blessed consciousness of His presence, power in service, or any other
spiritual gift, do not settle down, content to live without it,
but seek it diligently until you find. " Your hearts shall
live that seek God." If you have heard of some gift or
grace which others possess, and may be equally yours as
theirs, seek it. Seek it as men seek for hidden treasure or
for goodly pearls, or as the philosophers were wont to seek
for the substance which should turn everything into gold,
as explorers seek for the secret of the North Pole, or as
scientists search for the secrets which Nature holds back
from all but reverent and persevering inquiry. " Seek Him

that maketh the seven stars and Orion, and turneth the
shadow of death into the morning."

" He that seeketh, findeth." " If thou criest after knowledge, and liftest up thy voice for understanding; if thou
seekest her as silver, and searchest for her as for hid
treasures, then shalt thou understand the fear of the Lord,
and find the knowledge of God." We may not always find
just what we seek, but we shall come on something much
better, and more satisfying. Abraham and the patriarchs
declared plainly that they sought a country, but they all
died in tents, the shifting memorials of their pilgrimage.
The philosophers of the Middle Ages, to whom we have
referred, did not find the golden stone, but they laid the
foundations of modern chemistry. You may not obtain
that special opportunity of blessing others that you have
long desired ; but in your willingness to take a subordinate
position, in your meekness and humility, you will certainly
win a moral and spiritual influence incomparably greater.
The resolute seeker finds. He starts off to raise crops
of golden grain from the brown fields, and as patiently he
drives his plough, the metallic chink of the share on metal
makes it certain that he has come on treasure-trove.

(3) *Knock.* We ask for a gift; we seek something we have
lost; but we knock for admittance to the house of our
friend. A door stands between us and the master of the
house, which can only be opened from within. Then we
knock; at first quietly, and then more vehemently and
loudly, till we hear the drawing back of bolt and bar, and
see the door thrown open. We need the gifts of God, and
are thankful for the treasures which are to be obtained by
earnest, prayerful search ; but we should desire, above all,
to have face to face friendship with Himself. Sometimes
the door of fellowship stands wide open, and we can enter
without let or hindrance. At other times it seems as

though God had hidden His face and withdrawn Himself. These are the occasions when we must knock. And how often it has been the experience of the saints that, as they have stood waiting and knocking, the door has been opened as by an invisible hand, and the times of greatest difficulty at the beginning have been those of greatest liberty at the close !

"To him that knocketh it shall be opened." There is no doubt or hesitation in our Lord's assurance. In another paragraph He speaks of those who shall stand without and knock, saying, "Lord, Lord, open unto us," and He shall say, "Depart"; but that dread parable has nothing to do with the access into the presence of God, and the fellowship with God, of which the Master is here treating.  Persistency, urgency, the holy violence which will not be denied, are dear to the heart of God, and are certain to win a loving and favourable response.  "Though the vision tarry, wait for it: it shall come, it shall not tarry."

．　　．　　．　　．　　．　　．

AN ANALOGY. Bread and fish were the simple fare of the Galilean peasants whom our Lord addressed on the shores of their own beautiful lake—the bread as the necessary staff of life; the fish as an appetising addition.  Little children, in their simplicity, might sometimes mistake a stone for one of the small loaves of the Oriental shape and fashion, or a serpent for a fish.  But, even though the heart of a human father is fallen and evil, it cannot be supposed for an instant that he would give the child what it asked.  His love would at once withhold his hand. He would say: "No, little one, the stone is not food ; the serpent would sting and poison you: but, see, here is what you want—bread and fish.  I cannot give you *those*."  So it often happens that in this mortal life of ours, where the shadows fall so dense and dark, and we are obliged to grope in the twilight, we are hungry with immeasurable appetite, and think that this or the other boon will surely satisfy our souls. We clamour for a stone, thinking it to be bread ; or cry out for the glittering serpent, supposing it to be a dainty that will titillate our palate. But as the earthly father refused, notwithstanding his weakness and evil, much more will God refuse. " No," He says; " My child, I cannot, for love's sake, give it you; but, see, here is bread indeed, and here the fish—eat, drink, and be satisfied."

Again, God sometimes gives things that appear to be stones and serpents, but they turn out to be bread and fish. The mother of St. Augustine prayed to God that He would not suffer her beloved son to go to Rome, because she dreaded the persecutions which were threatening the city. He went, notwithstanding, and it was in Italy that he found Christ. Referring in after years to this incident in his life, he says : " What was it, O my God, that she sought of Thee with many tears ? Was it not that Thou wouldest not suffer me to to set sail for Rome ? But Thou, in Thy deep counsels, and listening to the hinge of her desire, didst disregard the thing which she asked for, that Thou mightest do in me that which she was ever asking—the conversion of my soul."

Do not be surprised if there are placed on your table viands that threaten to break your teeth and disagree with your digestion. Since God has put them there—and He is good—you will find them in the highest degree nutritious. Though they be the reverse of the prophet's vision—bitter to the mouth—they will prove to be wholesome, and sweet to the digestion.

Or take a third case. Suppose a child in its hunger asks for bread and fish. Its father, though evil, will not tantalise it by giving it something which will defy its powers of assimilation. Though he were to suffer the

extremities of starvation, he would cheerfully endure them
rather than respond thus to his child's artless faith. We
may therefore go with large requests to our God, asking
for what we need, and asking in the certain faith that He
will only give us good things. Each prayer we repeat will
be answered only in giving. He will substitute the blessing we would crave if we knew as much as He does of the
heart of man. What a comfort it is to know that God
gives only good things. What He withholds is good; what
He gives is good; what He substitutes in His answer to
our petitions is good—nay, good is not strong enough. He
gives always the best.

It should be remembered that our God gives not only
the necessaries, but the luxuries and comforts of life. The
Lord prepared for His hungry friends, exhausted by the
labours of the night, not bread alone, but fish. "When
they got out upon the land they see a fire of charcoal there,
and fish laid thereon, and bread." It was as though, in that
last breakfast with Him, the Master desired to teach that in
all coming time He would give His faithful disciples the
daily supply of their returning wants, together with the
warmth of human love, which ministers to the sense of
enjoyment as well as to present need.

This is a great consolation in prayer. We can ask for
anything and everything we want; we may be sure that
no good thing will be withholden from those who walk
uprightly; but we may also be sure that God loves us too
well to give anything that would hurt us.

Probably our lives are meagre and impoverished, when
they might become full of good things, because we fail to
ask. Notice our Lord's words: "How much more shall
your Father which is in heaven give good things to them
that ask Him." Is not the Apostle James right when He
says: "Ye have not because ye ask not?" That is the one

reason. Or, " Because ye ask amiss, that ye may consume it upon your lusts." That is the second reason. Either not to pray, or to pray from selfish motives, shuts us out of a great amount of Divine helpfulness which otherwise would be ours. Our Lord puts into our hands the key to the vaults in God's bank. It is our fault if all grace does not abound in us, and if we are poor when we might be rich.

.    .    .    .    .

An Injunction. "All things, therefore, whatsoever ye would that men should do unto you, even so do ye also unto them." With much reason this has been called " The Golden Rule."

Gibbon reminds us that, in a negative form, it was in vogue four centuries before the Christian Era. But this is not to be wondered at, since Christ was in the world from the first. " That was the true Light, even the Light which lighteth every man, coming into the world. He was in the world, and the world was made by Him, and the world knew Him not." But for the positive form of this truth, and for the power by which it can be made operative in our selfish, evil hearts, we are entirely indebted to the teaching and inspiration of Jesus Christ.

Translated into common English, this precept may be rendered: Put yourself in another's place; treat him as you would wish to be treated under similar circumstances; do not deal with him as you would not wish to be dealt with. The Lord, in effect, goes back to the words which stand at the beginning of the chapter, saying: " Judge as you would like to be judged; measure as you would like it to be measured to you."

The principle, of course, as He says, is witnessed " by the law and the prophets." We find it stated in the second great commandment: " Thou shalt love thy neighbour as thyself." It is *fundamental*, underpinning the whole structure of human society. It is *equitable*, because all men are more nearly on an equality than might be inferred from a consideration of their outward circumstances. It is *portable*, " like the two-foot rule " which the artisan carries in his pocket for the measurement of any work which he may be called to estimate.

The Emperor Severus was so charmed by the excellence of this rule that he ordered a crier to repeat it whenever he had occasion to punish any person, and he caused it to be inscribed on the most notable parts of the palace, and on many of the public buildings. But though the maxim has attracted so much attention and admiration, it is powerless to effect any great reform apart from the Holy Spirit. Therefore it is that in the other version of this paragraph, in Luke xi. 13, our Lord says : " How much more shall your heavenly Father give the Holy Spirit to them that ask Him ? " After all, it is only they who have stood under the open sky of Pentecost, who have received their share of that blessed enduement and infilling, which is the right of every believer—but which is too seldom claimed—who can go through the world practising always the golden rule of love. It is only they who by the Holy Spirit have been brought into living union with Christ, who receive hour by hour the full current of His life, that can go on loving men with the prodigality of affection—tempered, of course, with wisdom and discretion such as avail to fill up to the brim the full measure of the requirements of the Golden Rule. Let us simply, artlessly, and earnestly, ask our Father here and now to bestow upon us in His fulness this best of all donations—the Holy Spirit.

What a royal life this is to which our Master calls us—on the one hand, deriving all our needed resources from God ; and, on the other hand, therefore, able to be generous and free-handed to men. " He is able to make all grace abound towards us, that we, having all sufficiency in all things, may abound to every good work."

Too long have we given stones where men asked bread, and serpents where they asked fish. We have pelted men with stones, we have stung them with the poison of asps; and they have turned away from us and our religion with loathing. Henceforth let us go through life repeating in essence the wonderful miracle of John vi., where out of five barley loaves and two small fishes, broken by the hand of the Master, and distributed by the hand of the disciples, vast crowds of hungry people were satisfied. Take your bread and fish from Christ, and then break and give—*break and give!* There will always be twelve baskets full of fragments left for your personal need.

## XX.

# Counterfeits—"Beware!"
### (MATT. vii. 13–27.)

THE world is full of counterfeits, and shams abound! Too often we paint and varnish paper to look like marble; we make paste jewels; we make of paper the soles of boots; and experts are deceived. There is great danger, therefore, of the same spirit creeping into the Church; and our Lord, who knew the heart of man, warns His disciples against the counterfeits of true religion.

. . . . . .

That Religious Experience is a Counterfeit which DOES NOT INVOLVE THE DENIAL OF SELF. We must distinguish between the denial of self and self-denial. There may be self-denial which, so far from being the denial of self, leads to self-congratulation and self-aggrandisement. The daughter of a fashionable home may elect to forego the gossip around the afternoon tea in her mother's drawing-room, in order to visit an East-End slum, but in her heart of hearts she may be exulting in an afternoon's freedom from conventional custom; she may be congratulating herself on the admiration which her presence may excite amongst the poor; she may be desirous of building up a reputation, and of extracting pity for her self-denying labours. In all this there is a subtle ministering to self, which is not easy to detect; but there is no symptom of the spirit of the Cross, the Strait Gate is not entered, the Narrow Way is not trodden. The religious spirit, which is of great price in God's sight, must cut deep into the tap-root of our self-life.

Every religion has recognised this. A non-Christian Hindu told me at Calcutta that Hinduism demanded eight different steps in the elimination of the self-life, beginning with the love of woman and ending with the love of money. The Greeks recited the story of the Choice of Hercules, that when his young manhood was budding he was assailed by Venus and Minerva—the former promising that she would lead him by a short and easy path to the enjoyment of all delights; whilst the latter, as Leonardo depicts her, demure and staid, in her dress of grey, offered him the stern tasks of duty, calling him to forego the life of self-indulgence. In Hebrew apocryphal literature there is nothing more beautiful than the sketch in the book of Esdras, of the city, "full of all manner of good things," standing in the midst of a wide plain, entered by a single narrow portal, which could only be reached by crossing a narrow causeway—so narrow that only one could walk alone—with a raging fire on the right hand and storm-swept water on the left. Every religion which has touched the heart of man has bidden him enter in by "the Strait Gate."

The Lord's picture is very graphic. Each fresh generation seems to stand in a large, open valley, full of hope and eager expectation; and each unit fully intending to make the best of the brief spell of human existence, which is all that is granted, and without the opportunity of returning for a second trial. There are two avenues by which that valley may be left; and our Lord proceeds to contrast the two gates, the character and breadth of the two ways, the number of travellers that frequent them, and their respective goals.

The most popular of these two gates is one that rears its

lofty height in white marble, fair and glistening, whose ample space admits a never-ceasing procession of gay young forms, which fill the air with their songs and beat the earth with their dancing feet. Festoons of ivy and vine leaves are carved in the living stone, and gates that look like burnished gold stand wide. It opens on a gently sloping sward, enamelled with flowers and crossed by devious tracks; now and again the path expands into open spaces and woodland glades; but as furlong follows furlong the grass becomes barer, the flowers fewer, the track itself is less defined, the crowds become broken up into smaller and smaller groups, and these dissolve into individuals, until finally each finds himself in a land of pits and precipices, where destruction threatens at every step, whilst darkness which may be felt casts midnight shadows. No voice answers to the voice that piteously cries for help; no hand is stretched out to catch the hand that reaches out for succour. How "wide is the gate and broad is the way that leadeth to destruction, and many there be that go in thereat."

But in that valley there is another aperture—a Wicket Gate, that might easily be missed unless looked for; this is so narrow that only one can enter at a time, divested of every encumbrance. The path, at the head of which this straight entrance stands, is at first steep and difficult, paved with flints which cut the tender feet. It climbs the bleak hillside—on the one hand the beetling cliffs, on the other the deep ravine, and only a ledge to walk on. It is trodden, not by crowds, but by individuals. The idea of Christiana and her children is truer in the realm of fancy than in fact. But the end is glorious, for that path breaks out at last upon the uplands, "where God Himself is Sun."

(1) *The entrance to the life of discipleship demands an effort.* "The gate is strait." We need not work for forgiveness;

this is ours by the free grace of God.    We are not to work
for salvation, but from it.    We do not work to be saved; but,
being saved, we work.    There must be effort to relinquish—
effort to be still, and to await the strong hand of our Lord,
lifting us up from the brink of despair.    To lay aside every
weight, to refuse the tendency to self-effort, to turn one's
back resolutely on some darling sin, and one's face towards
the New Jerusalem, to choose the path of separation and
service—these call for effort, which our Lord compares to
the passage of a strait gate.    You cannot drive into it in a
carriage, or carry through it your money-bags and your
weights.

(2) *The continuance in the path of discipleship demands
continuous effort.*    "Narrow is the way."    The world's
religion is easy enough.    "Do as you like," is its
motto.    "Be not righteous over much," is its law.
You may go to church, undertake some branch of religious
philanthropy, and observe certain fasts and festivals—
only it must be at the dictate of your own whim, and
be for your own self-pleasing.    The path of the disciple, on the other hand, is one of perpetual limitation
and restraint.    He does not his own will, but the will of
Him that sent him.    He anoints his head, and washes his
face, not appearing to men to fast; but all the time he is
under the strict law of Christ, which, because it is the law
of love, is the most inexorable law of all.

*The upward path is lonely.    Few* there be that find it.
In the days when Christianity has been most popular the
real disciples have been fewest.    Always "a little flock."
Always "not many" are called.    God called Abram when
he was but one.

(3) But *the end is absolutely glorious*, and more than com-
pensates.    They that tread that path, saying "No" to self,
because they are always saying "Yes" to Christ, leave

behind the valleys where the miasma broods, and climb to
the upland levels of life. They do not need to wait for
the end of their journey to realize God's full gift of life ;
but here and now, at each step and each moment, as they
are faithful to death, God gives them a crown of life ; as
they are always delivered unto death for Jesus' sake, the
life of Jesus becomes more and more manifest in their
mortal bodies. Each step forward is into purer atmosphere
and further vision. " It leadeth unto life."

.    .    .    .    .    .

That Religious Experience is a Counterfeit which
DOES NOT PRODUCE GOOD FRUIT. Our Lord applies this
principle, first, to *false guides*. It was natural that, from
speaking of the gate and way, He should go on to charac-
terise the guides, who profess to be able to guide the
pilgrim feet by the right track to the right goal. He says,
in effect, *Do not judge by appearances*, for they are very
deceptive. The *wolf*, which comes to ravin, may don the
fleece of a sheep ; *thorns* may produce a little black berry,
which, in the early spring, resembles the black grape ;
*thistles* of a certain description will have a blossom not
altogether unlike the fig-tree. " By their fruits ye shall
know them."

Primarily this does not mean that the doctrine is the
tree, but the man who teaches the doctrine ; and you can
detect his true nature, not by remarking his words and acts
when he is conscious of being watched by many eyes, but
by the silent and unconscious fruit of temper, disposition,
behaviour, in the privacy of the home or amid the obscurity
of daily common places. A good tree bringeth forth good
fruit ; an evil tree cannot bring forth good fruit.

But it may be replied, Are there not many amongst us
who refuse the doctrines of the New Testament, but whose
lives and characters condemn many Evangelical professors ?

Does not the presence of such persons in our midst disprove these words of our Lord, and prove that the life is no true test of doctrine? No; because the very atmosphere we breathe is saturated with Christian and Evangelical influences. We all owe more to our mothers than we know. The good in the persons whose case we are considering proves that they come of a godly stock, or had, like Lord Shaftesbury, a devoted governess or nurse, or came under the influence of a Christian schoolmaster. As boys they may have been taken to hear the truth as it is in Jesus, proclaimed by lips forever sealed in death. To borrow the thought of another—the momentum that carries the train continues long after the driver has turned off the steam; the tidal wave moves onward long after it has left the attraction of the moon; the radiance of the dying day lingers on the horizon long after the sun has set.

On the whole, the worth and truth of the Gospel have been abundantly attested all down the ages, by the myriads of noble characters it has produced, which have been as salt to the world's corruption and as lights in its darkness.

It is a solemn question for every teacher amongst us: "Am I bearing good or evil fruit? What is the impression which I am producing on those around me? Am I a fruit-bearing branch in the True Vine? If not, whatever my doctrine may be, I am running a serious risk of being cut down and cast into the fire." To save us from that fate, it is not enough to teach others the conditions of fruit-bearing, not enough to refrain from bearing evil fruit, not enough to be a neutral or negative quantity—the failure to bring forth good fruit will cause us to be condemned to the axe and the bonfire. Many of those who condemn others for their heterodoxy, and pride themselves on the straitness and strictness of their adherence to Evangelical doctrine, but who in their criticism of others betray a terrible deficiency of Christian love, and in their domestic life give no signs of the sweetness and humility of Christ, will find some day that their fervid zeal for orthodoxy of creed, which has not been accompanied by orthodoxy of character and conduct, has not availed to secure them from the fate meted out to worthless fruit-trees.

Our Lord applies the same principle, next, to *false professors*. He shows how far a man may go and be lost. He may have a considerable amount of reverence and respect for the Lord's name. He is depicted as addressing the Master as " Lord, Lord "; and as avowing, three times over, that the name of Christ has been the talisman and charm by the use of which all the miracles and mighty works have been accomplished. Three classes defile before us, only to be rejected at the judgment-seat of Christ, where those eyes which are as a flame of fire pierce the counterfeit disciple through and through. First come the prophets, not in the sense of *fore*-telling, but of *forth*-telling, the message of a salvation which they have never appropriated for themselves. Next come the exorcists, who have cast demons out of all others than themselves. Lastly come the wonder-workers. But each of these classes is turned away. Not only does the King not know them as they approach, but He professes unto them that He never did know them, and that their works have been works of iniquity. Every work which is wrought in the spirit of vainglory, and for the sake of securing a personal reward, is accounted as nothing by the Master, yea, as worse than nothing—it is an affront to Him. Its doer flouts His mercy and long-suffering, and acts as though He had never shed His blood, never expiated his sins, never purchased his redemption. Do those who eulogise the sublime morality of this discourse, but refuse to admit the Divine claims of the Speaker, read these closing words? If so, how do they understand them? Does the sanity which has characterised the Master's utterances hitherto forsake them now? Is He reliable as a Teacher and Guide only in dealing with the difficult problems of human life, becoming a mere visionary when, without one word of explanation or apology, He assumes the right to sit upon the judgment-seat and utter the verdict of eternity on the quick and dead? If we accept the one set of utterances as the very essence of truth, why should we draw the line when He speaks as able to bid these false disciples to depart?

This is He with whom you and I have to do; and, I pray you, make sure work for eternity. If you are wrong it is surely better to find out your mistake here and now rather than after the die is cast. You may speak with the tongues of men and angels, give all your goods to feed the poor, and your body to be burned in your steadfast witness to the truth—but if you are not inspired by a Divine love to God and man it will count for nothing; and when once the Master has shut-to the door, it will be in vain for you to stand without and knock, saying, "Open to us." The door will not open. The darkness will not be riven by a shaft of ruddy light issuing from within. The stern rejection will not be succeeded by a loving recognition.

Do you fear lest such a fate should be yours? Then be of good cheer. Those that dread it most are safest from it. Those who are most self-confident have most reason for alarm. "Not every one that *saith* unto me, Lord, Lord, shall enter into the Kingdom of heaven, but he that *doeth* the will of My Father which is in heaven." There is no need to die before we can enter it; but here and now, as we with many fears and failures set ourselves to do God's will, we may enter the Kingdom, and become citizens of its metropolis—the New Jerusalem which comes down out of heaven from God being radiant with His glory.

.    .    .    .    .    .

That Religious Experience is a Counterfeit which DOES NOT SECURE CONTACT BETWEEN THE SOUL AND CHRIST, WITH A FAITH LEADING TO OBEDIENCE. In any of those Syrian valleys, which some may have visited, between Beyrout and Damascus, it is possible to see wrought out the ´closing picture of His sermon. In the summer the soil is baked and hard with the intense heat, and any spot will serve equally well as the site of a house. No one can say whether his neighbour has built well or ill; and only the builder himself knows.

But in the winter all is altered. The country is then exposed to sudden and heavy storms. The stiff breeze drives up the rain-clouds from the Mediterranean, which empty themselves in floods of rain, and suddenly the water-courses, which for months had been little better than heaps of stones, are filled with foaming floods from bank to brae, pouring down into the valleys and carrying all before them.

It goes ill, under such circumstances, with the man who has pitched his slightly-constructed house on the sand, taking no heed to dig down to the rock beneath, for the foundations are sapped by the rushing torrent, and the very sand is swept into new banks and beds. But the builder who has excavated to the living rock, and grappled it in the lowest courses of his construction, can look without dismay at the scene of devastation around. It comes not nigh to him; only with his eyes does he behold and see the doom of the unwary.

Such is the contrast between the man who hears and does not heed, and him who hears, ponders, and obeys. For, in the words of the Apostle: " Not the hearers of the

law are just before God, but the doers of the law shall be
justified " (Rom. ii. 13).

What searching words are these. We have all heard,
but have we done? Are we hearers that forget, or doers
that work? Do we continue in the perfect law of liberty?
Have we ever come into personal and living contact with
that " Stone, that tried Stone, that precious Corner-stone,"
which God has laid before the worlds were made, for a sure
foundation? *To believe about Christ is not enough; we
must believe in Him.* We must come to Him as a Living
Stone, and be made living stones (1 Peter ii. 4–8). Then,
and in the impulses received from Him through the Holy
Spirit, we shall proceed to build the structure of a godly
and holy character, not with wood, hay, and stubble, but
with gold, silver, and precious stones, and it shall grow
unto a holy temple in the Lord (1 Cor. iii. 10–15).

Is it to be wondered at that the people felt that the
Master's words were fraught with a mysterious authority
and power which were absent from the words of all other
speakers? All men have borne witness to this same
characteristic, which adds the greater condemnation to
those who reject, but which communicates the pulse and
thrill of the Divine Spirit to those who receive with meekness the engrafted Word that is able to save the soul.